A Question-and-Answer Book for Families

"The family is the basic unit of society. To a great extent, our understanding of the Bible is based on a proper understanding of the family. If God had felt that proper family life was impossible, I don't believe he would have put us together and told us to live in family groups.

"I offer these observations to you as the gift of my experience, and simply trust that they'll be of some encouragement to some families."

—Jay Kesler

"I WANT A HOME WITH NO PROBLEMS"

JAY KESLER

A Key-Word Book
Word Books, Publisher
Waco, Texas

First Key-Word edition—February 1981

I Want a Home with No Problems

Copyright © 1977 by Word Incorporated
Waco, Texas 76703

Printed in the United States of America

ISBN 0-8499-4154-7

Library of Congress Catalog Card Number: 77-83339

Contents

Part Two. Parent/Child Relationships: Parents Are People, Too!

**Part Three.   Extended Family Relationships: In–laws
and Out–laws**

**Part Four.   Interpersonal Relationships: Who Is My
Neighbor?**

**Part Five.   Family Finances: Where Does All the
Money Go?**

Part Seven.   College: To Go or Not to Go?

Bibliography of Recommended Books

Preface

I encourage you to approach this book as you would a cafeteria. Don't feel you must pick up everything and eat it. On the other hand, if something doesn't look appetizing now, maybe the next time through it will. Nonetheless, feel absolutely free to go through the line and make up your own mind. You may decide that you'd rather go to another restaurant down the street!

This is a question and answer book—and I make no apology for that. It grew out of questions from listeners to Youth for Christ's "Family Forum" radio broadcast heard daily on stations all across America. The many hundreds of questions received tend to fall into categories, which made me realize that our human problems are universal.

The primary tool of the enemy of our soul is to make us feel isolated, as if our problem is ours alone. Not so. In the same sense the Scripture says, "There hath no temptation taken you but such is common to man" (1 Cor. 10:13). Our problems tend to be common. As we understand this commonality and the fact that we are working through life together, the experiences of other people can be a source of counsel, joy, and instruction. Through the experiences of others we begin to find light for our particular situation.

I'm very opposed to being the "answer man," the know-it-all approach. I just don't feel comfortable in that role. In fact, I answer most questions with a question, because I have strong feelings that each individual problem belongs to an individual person. There are so many variables in each situation that it becomes virtually impossible to find blanket solutions to someone else's problems.

On the other hand, as one lives his or her life, he does learn certain lessons. I have often looked to others with experience in marriage or family relationships to give me counsel. Some are hesitant for fear I'll come back later and say, "You gave me bad advice." If this were true in all areas of life, no one would ever pass on advice or information. In a sense, every generation would have to touch its own stove to see if it's hot. There would be no progress in history. We would all have to start from ground zero and build our own set of experiences.

For this reason I've taken on the task of attempting to provide insights from the experience I've gained in more than twenty years of youth work in Youth for Christ. I see myself as an interpreter, interpreting adults to youth, and youth to adults, working with the Christian family. In a sense, I am also a mediator between the two.

There's no guarantee that my answers will apply to you. I offer these observations to you as the gift of my experience, and simply trust that they'll be of some encouragement and some blessing to readers, especially families. The family is the basic unit of society. To a great extent, our understanding of the Bible, God's revelation to us, is based on a proper understanding of the family. If God felt that proper family life was impossible I don't believe He would have put us together in families and told us to live in family groups. I believe there are solutions.

On the other hand, I don't believe there is a solution to every problem. I believe there are directions and attitudes and climates in which solutions best take place.

So I am not presenting this book as a know-it-all who feels he's arrived and can now tell you how to do it. Rather, I am a fellow pilgrim who lives in a very typical home with successes and failures. Janie and I have been married twenty years. We have three teen-agers in our home, one going off to college this fall. We've had successes and failures, but together we can all conclude it's been a good experience. We're grateful to our God for the privilege of having this experience together.

And so with a sense of humility and good humor, and a great feeling of responsibility toward you, we present this book as a kind of cafeteria. Eat what you can; don't feel you have to eat everything on your plate. If something doesn't appeal to you, pass it by. It is my hope that in all of these items on the "menu" there will be a full meal for those who take the time to read this book.

I want to express special thanks to Al Bryant who helped me put these questions and answers in book form. Words come easily to me, but he has helped put them into a style easy for others to read and understand.

Jay Kesler

Husband/Wife Relationships

Part One.

After You've Said I Do

Love Should Grow . . .

I'm a twenty–five–year–old housewife. I've been married one and a half years. My husband and I are anxious to build a strong Christian home, but neither of us feels our love for each other is what it should be. We're praying about it and hope you can send us some guidelines to help our love grow. Any suggestions you can send will be an answer to prayer.

I like your phrase—love should grow. That is exactly what must happen with love. It is a small acorn that grows into a large oak. Many people I meet seem to feel that marriage reaches its apex at the honeymoon and then goes downhill. Not so.

I can remember seeking advice from Christian friends when my wife and I began our marriage. Many people gave us advice. But one of my favorite friends sat down with me and made the comment, "Forget about yourself." That to me has been the best advice I've received. See the other person as someone to build your life around—make him or her the center of your life. This begins to build a real love relationship that grows and grows.

Interestingly enough, when the Bible speaks about love, it speaks about something entirely different from our concept of love today: *I love someone*—meaning I feel all fuzzy, as if I'm standing in pajamas with feet in them! In the Bible, love is not a feeling or emotion as much as something you do.

I went through 1 Corinthians 13, listing some negative things about love.

Paul says love is not jealous; love is not boastful, proud, selfish, or rude. It doesn't demand its own way or hold grudges. Then on the positive side—love is patient, kind, and loyal. It believes the best about the other person, and it stands its ground in defending the other person. These are action things we can do toward our mate—and as we do these things, our love grows.

These four words added to our marriage vocabulary would help: 1. *Affirmation*—seek ways to affirm each other, 2. *Vulnerability*—open ourselves first so that the other person is able to open himself, 3. *Honesty*—share how we really feel in given situations, 4. *Communication*—talk to each other—spend time together each day and let each other know what is going on inside. These actions will cause love to grow.

Where Does the Time Go?

When is the best time for a husband and wife to discuss things? When my husband comes home I'm busy getting the kids organized and preparing our evening meal. When the meal is over, he reads while I do the dishes. The next few hours are spent getting the kids ready to go to bed. By that time I have to do some other chores like a load of wash or mopping. When we go to bed I'm so tired I don't feel like talking. In the morning, it's rushing through breakfast and off to work. On Saturdays, my husband has his special duties. Sunday is full of church activities. There just doesn't seem to be any time to discuss problems where we evaluate our progress as husband and wife, and as parents. What do other people do?

Well, most people do what you are doing. They complain about it and feel trapped by their busy schedules. We're all living on some sort of a merry–go–round. The ponies are going around too fast, and we can't ride them all! But there is a note in your letter that bothers me—a problem I've encountered many times. That is, when people have cleared their schedules and have found time for each other, they discover there's nothing to talk about—they have nothing in common. They've been so busy working they've forgotten how to court each other!

One of the most important things in marriage is courtship. That courtship ought to continue during marriage, not just go on before marriage. Courtship is communicating. It is getting to know the other person.

Now, let me suggest some solutions to your problem. Instead of your husband reading while you do the dishes, how about the two of you doing the dishes together? Talk while you are doing them. This would be one time you could do two things at once!

Another possibility: get up a little earlier. I know many busy people who resolve the togetherness problem this way. Have a leisurely cup of coffee before the children are up—just for the sheer enjoyment of being together. Read a chapter from the Bible together and pray for God's guidance through the day. You will be amazed how many more hours there are in the day if you give part of it to the Lord, and start the day in this way.

In addition, I believe you ought to have some special time as a couple—lunch, for instance, on a Saturday. You may say you can't afford it. How about McDonald's? Have something to eat and look at each other. Talk and just spend some special time together. Every couple ought to get out together at least once a month, just the two of them—not with another couple. They need to look across the table at each other, enjoying one another, and learn to show interest in each other—not as a sex partner or as someone who does the dishes, or someone who earns the income, but as a person, another human being.

One final word: it sounds like your children are small. They will be older someday. The day will come when they will get themselves ready for bed! Look forward to that day with anticipation—but learn to enjoy each other today!

What About Submission?

My wife and I went to a seminar for young married couples and enjoyed it very much. We were richly blessed by the practical guidelines offered—at least I thought we were. But I don't think my wife has taken the part about submission seriously enough. Before we went to the seminar I knew something was wrong with our marriage, but I didn't know what. Now I know it was lack of submission. How do I get my wife to realize this?

Without sounding as if I'm not taking your letter seriously—let me say, you can lead a horse to water, but you can't make him drink! There's a great difference between knowing something and doing it. You can go to a seminar and be told that wives ought to submit themselves, but if the wife isn't ready for that truth, then she doesn't hear it. I would suspect a great many marriages have this particular problem—wives and husbands haven't understood the chain of command taught in the Scriptures. For instance, Ephesians 5 talks about wives submitting themselves to husbands. Husbands like to read that to their wives, but they don't read on a little further where it says, "Husbands, love your wives as Christ loves the church," or, "Husbands, love your wives as you love your own body."

I'm convinced that the Bible is the most impartial and balanced guidebook we've ever had. It tells us to honor father and mother; it instructs us not to provoke children to wrath. But don't allow God's Book to become a bludgeon for one person to use on another! There is a fairness in it all.

Maybe your wife thinks the problem lies somewhere else—that you've just decided she hasn't submitted to you. Perhaps you should sit down together and see what she learned at the seminar. Two people can attend the same seminar and come away with two different impressions. Ask her what she heard. It is possible she thinks there is another problem.

Both of you have to be ready to discuss what was said. There is a vast difference between a woman who believes in authority and one who is rebelling against authority. The first can later repent and say, "Well, Lord, that's where I've been wrong. I'm sorry. I'm wrong and I'm going to submit myself to my husband." It's quite another situation if the woman doesn't believe in authority or is having a struggle with whether Paul really understood twentieth century women. That's a whole different matter. Don't simply raise the volume on the advice given as you understood it. Sit quietly with your wife and find out what she really heard. Submission may not be the problem at all. It may simply be a breakdown in communication between you.

My Wife Is a Gossip . . .

My wife is a terrible gossip, and I don't know what to do to get her to stop. It is such a frustrating thing for me. I can't even trust her with certain things about my work and my friends—even things at church. I love her so much, and feel that a wall is developing between us in this area. Do you have any suggestions?

I'd start on the wall—the wall that exists between you is a wall of distrust. That is, you are unable to trust your wife because she has shown herself untrustworthy. I'd confront her with this and say, "Honey, I do love you—you know I do, but we have this problem. We cannot really have the kind of love and fellowship and communion with each other we ought to have because of your inability to handle private information."

At this point, of course, you've made the right choice—that

is, not to share everything. Some people simply cannot bear the weight of information—they can't handle it. A person who cannot bear the weight of confidentiality should not have to deal with it. Explain to her that her inability to bear this weight of confidential information is building a wall between you. You'll probably find she is as anxious as you are to break down that wall.

As you get into this discussion, you might ask her why she gossips. She'll probably bluster at first and say, "Well, it's not really gossip—it's information." If she is a Christian, I suggest you read specific scriptures where we are told we shouldn't gossip, that gossip is a sin. If she isn't a Christian, I'd help her to understand that gossip hurts others, and we don't have the right to hurt other people with our tongues. The tongue is a weapon—the Bible calls it an unruly evil, a deadly poison. To help her to understand this will be of some help.

Usually people gossip for one of two reasons. Some gossip because they want to have the inside track—they want to say to others, I am special, I am important, I know things other people don't know. Therefore I have importance. That is one reason for gossip, and this may be your wife's reason.

There is another group who gossip for a much more complex reason. They are attempting to justify or confirm their own actions. Deep down they are dissatisfied with themselves. So, they have to constantly point out faults in other people, saying more or less, "I'm bad, but I'm just as good as this person."

What we must do is get to the root of the problem—to realize that each of us is forgiven and accepted by God. Because I'm bad but still accepted by God, this person then, about whom I'm tempted to gossip—yes, of course he's bad, but he is also accepted and forgiven by God. In *Screwtape Letters* C. S. Lewis says, "If I being what I know myself to be can call myself a Christian, why can't this person being what he seems to be, call himself the same name?" When you can accept that, then you can find the source, root, and spigot to cut off the gossip.

I Need More Attention . . .

This is rather a personal problem, but I just wasn't sure where to turn for help. We've been married four years and have a beautiful two–year–old son. We're quite happy, but my wife seems to be so wrapped up in taking care of Jamie, I'm sort of left out in the cold. At night she's worn out and even when I just want her to sit with me for a while, she has to be jumping up and checking on the baby all the time. It's not that I'm jealous, but how do I tell her that maybe I need a little more attention?

This question often comes up when a new baby enters a household. Sometimes the family dog can't adjust to the lack of attention—or an older child. Here is a husband who has a very real problem. I can hear what you're saying and I understand it. Many men get married without realizing there will have to be adjustments in wedded life. In *Death of a Salesman* Willie Loman makes this comment about selling: "It comes with the territory." He is talking about pain, hurt, and so on. There are certain things that come with marriage, and one thing, of course, is responsibility.

A child in the home demands time. Perhaps your son at two years old is learning how to run the home. Children learn very early and decide who is going to be in control. And usually children decide before the parents do! They follow a cause–and–effect philosophy—if they cry, they can get attention; if they don't, nothing happens. So they learn that if you make a fuss, you can get someone to come to you.

This reminds me of a cartoon. There are two white mice. One says to the other, "I think I'm getting the scientist conditioned. Every time I go through this little door, he gives me a piece of cookie." A child can do that to a parent as well. May I suggest that you and your wife sit down and talk about it. She should understand that you do need a little more attention. Maybe the two of you need to take a new approach toward Jamie. A child can play alone and he even needs to cry it out occasionally. Then he will learn his toys are just as much fun as his mother. Maybe together you can put a few restrictions on him and not let him run the household.

He should not be allowed to drive a wedge between you and your wife. You are his parents—and it is vitally important to his welfare that the two of you have a good relationship.

My Wife Looks Like a Wreck . . .

Here's my problem: every day when I get home my wife looks like a wreck. It's terrible—curlers, jeans, old sweatshirt. I realize she's busy around the house all day, and I don't expect her to look like a beauty queen. But if only she'd straighten herself up a little, she'd be much more appealing. What's your opinion?

I'm not sure I want to get in the middle between you! Your letter says it, doesn't it? We've all heard of this kind of thing —someone feeling this way about his or her spouse. I've heard women talk the same way about their husbands: when he comes home from work he puts on his oldest clothes. He sits there in a chair like a lump and doesn't say anything! This problem is common in marriage.

The kindest and best thing would be for the husband to say to his wife in this situation, "Honey, this bothers me." She will probably bluster a little and tell you how hard she works. How can you expect her to do all these things? Afterward I suppose she might change some of her behavior a little bit. She also might become more resentful.

The deeper problem in this sort of situation is that often rather than speaking to his wife about the difficulty straight on, the husband develops a sense of resentment and begins to show it in other ways. He'll cool off toward his wife, criticize her in other areas, give her the silent treatment. He may even get involved in some extramarital relationship because he feels his wife is no longer interested in him.

I'm assuming that your wife's particular problem is based on carelessness. Perhaps she's become so used to having you around she feels she doesn't need to dress up. That's a bad situation. As I've said before, courtship should continue throughout marriage. To the degree that it does, a couple will be more satisfied and happier with one another.

On the other hand, this problem may be caused by a lack of self-respect, by the wife feeling she no longer has a meaningful position in the world—she's just a housewife. There's no such thing as being just a housewife! Everyone has a place in God's plan. Being a wife, mother, and homemaker is one of the most important careers a woman can follow. So try affirmation. Whenever she is doing something you like, whenever she looks particularly sharp, compliment her. Affirm her, and you'll discover she will begin to respond to you positively.

My Wife Is a Slow Starter . . .

My wife and I played it straight before we were married, so I had no way of knowing what a slow starter she is in the morning. Boy, was I surprised! The honeymoon wasn't so bad, but as soon as we returned home. . . . I got up the first day to go to work, but she wouldn't get up. "You can get something at Dunkin' Doughnuts, can't you?" she asked. I couldn't believe it. All my life my mother has been up, dressed, breakfast ready, and things popping from the time the alarm went off. Is this something I'm going to have to live with the rest of my life?

When I first started thinking about this letter, I was going to answer "probably." We've all heard about hawks and doves. How about owls and sparrows? Some people are more alert at night, while some function better during the daytime. When you get a night person and a day person together, you have a challenge. I'm not saying it's insurmountable.

First, acknowledge the fact that you don't think she measures up well to your memory of your mother in the morning. For her part, she may find you a little dull in the evening! As soon as the sun goes down, you begin to look for the roost. She probably thinks you're a strange bird, too. So you have to get this out in the open. There is the reality of work—and the resentment of having to get up to do it. Some of us just don't like to look at that shower nozzle and say, "Wow, another day!"

It might be good to develop a schedule that allows your wife to have some time to herself earlier in the evening. It might work out this way: she has the responsibilities of fixing meals, doing dishes, cleaning the house. By the time she gets that all done, you're pretty well ready to go to bed. So that's all you have to do—watch the news and go to bed. She needs some time to unwind—everyone needs time for meditation, a little quiet time. Maybe you can change the whole evening schedule a little by helping her with some of her chores so she can get to bed a little earlier. Maybe then she will be able to get up in the morning. Don't expect her to get up smiling and run around the house! It probably isn't going to be.

How about trying to be day people during the week and night people on the weekends? Some couples have found this arrangement works for them. The husband who is used to getting up during the week sleeps in and stays up a little later on the weekend. No matter how hard you work at it, you will need some time to synchronize your internal time clocks. Most of all, you need a joint commitment to do it. Conquer your problem together.

We Aren't Compatible . . .

My husband and I have been married for a little over three years. While our problem isn't unique, I have no idea what to do about it. After living together for three years, we have discovered we don't share the same interests. It's almost humorous how opposite we are. He is an avid political observer—he may even run for office some day. He likes country music. He reads a great deal, but it's mostly sports and news magazines. He also watches TV a lot. I think politics, sports (especially cars), and country music are a waste of time, and I've told him so. That was a mistake, I think. Anyway, our life together is rapidly deteriorating, and I don't know what to do. Now please don't ask me why I didn't think of these things before I married him. Even if I knew the answer, that wouldn't help the present situation. What I want to know is, what can I do now?

If we find an answer to your problem, we should put it out in book form. There would be a real market for it! This matter of incompatibility between couples is a major marital problem. You warned me not to say, "Why did you get into this in the first place?" Tragically, many people who aren't married yet, but are only contemplating marriage, haven't even thought of the problem of incompatibility. There are many people married who would be much happier single because they are married to the wrong person.

I like to think of marriage as a triangular arrangement—Christ at the top, the apex, and each marriage partner as the legs. The closer we get to Christ, the closer we get to one another. This is really true. You have to build compatibility on a commitment you each made to the other.

You haven't mentioned anything about your Christian faith, so I'd guess this doesn't have a paramount place in your life. I don't feel a really good marriage can be built without God. You have to have a common place of meeting—a universal agreement as to what is right and what your goals are. God is the only One who can engineer that.

On a strictly human level, let me suggest this. You did make a mistake by telling your husband his interests are a waste of time. Try to figure out why he chooses those interests rather than being with you. Perhaps, in his mind at least, you've become less interesting, less attractive, and less fun— it may be your nagging is making it even worse. I'd suggest that you sit down with him and simply express to him that though you cannot share some of the things he enjoys, and he apparently can't share some of your interests, you're going to have to find a third area which both of you can enjoy. The solution to your problem is going to involve give and take on the part of both of you. Spend some time in that third area and develop it if you desire to bring your marriage together. Also, go to a competent marriage counselor, or your pastor. Learn how you can begin to find a mutual area of interest where you can get together as husband and wife. Since you haven't mentioned a common interest in church and related activities, I'd recommend that you make a joint effort in that direction. God is the only One who can create compatibility!

My Husband Was Unfaithful . . .

A couple of years ago my husband was unfaithful to me. He broke it off with the other woman before I knew anything about it, and confessed it all to me. He is a good husband and I love him very much, but I just can't forget about his deceitfulness. I'm always afraid he will fool me again. He always tells me he loves me and would never do it again. I want to forget about it, but I can't. My attitude hurts him very much, and it hurts me.

Yours is a difficult problem. Let's face it—adultery exists in the Christian family. Sin is sin and it does leave deep scars. But remember this as well: the blood of Christ cleanses us from all sin. Marital infidelity is not unwashable. Christ can and does forgive this sin.

We're thinking about forgiveness on several levels here, however. First John 1:9 tells us: "If we confess our sins, he is faithful and just to forgive us our sins, and to cleanse us from all unrighteousness." It's marvelous that the grace of God is able to find us no matter how far down we are, and forgive us. I'm sure your husband is grateful for this, and you're both grateful that he's been forgiven by God. Next is the forgiveness that must come between you. It seems you have forgiven each other, and your husband is dealing with forgiving himself. As so many of us do, he wants to punish himself. We don't like to let Christ die on the cross for our sins—we want to make a sacrifice and do something to prove ourselves.

I detect something further, and that is the healing of the memory—your own mind. The devil can work. He is powerful, and he uses tools, often very subtly. For instance, he's saying to you, what kind of woman are you that your husband needs to go off with another woman? You feel insecure and rejected. The devil will use that feeling, and he'll come around and tempt you at that level to make you feel inadequate. Know this: you will never get to the place where this fact of your husband's sin will be an un–fact. It will always be in your memory. But know this: when Christ forgives, and your husband forgives, you too must forgive. The two of you must work this out with the Lord.

Paul told us to forget those things that are behind. Perhaps the two of you need to go to your pastor. Sit down together and pray it through. Talk it through and resolve it before the Lord. Be thankful that 1 John 1:9 is still in the Bible!

My Husband Ought to Be the Spiritual Leader . . .

I really want ours to be a Christian home, but I can't do it by myself. I know the husband ought to be the spiritual leader of the home, but I just can't get him to be. He goes to church all right, but when it comes to family devotions, or even talking about things of the Spirit, he leaves it all to me. I don't want to talk to him about it because he'd think I was being pushy.

First of all, I think you *should* talk to him—hiding things from your husband and talking to someone else about your problem is a little bit unfair. You can tell him what your concerns are without being pushy or nagging. Whether he'll feel those concerns are legitimate is another question.

The concept of a woman's being the lone spiritual leader in the home is not a new idea really. Look at the New Testament. Some women's names are quite prominent there: Lydia, Mary, Martha, and so on. These women were taking spiritual leadership. These ladies must have been pretty dominant and strong.

Just what is spiritual leadership? Each of us has in his mind a model of what the ideal Christian husband or wife should be, so we're expecting our husband or wife to live up to that particular model, rather than the model of the Bible. Perhaps we have picked up something from a Christian movie or a Christian leader—and we say, "If only my husband could get to be like that." The truth is there are some men whose piety is private—so deep and personal that they feel to bring it out in the open would be irreverent. They may keep their spiritual concerns within themselves.

It isn't necessarily true that a verbal person is the most spiritual person. Perhaps your husband is saying things to your children that aren't being said by a husband who chatters all the time. For instance, Scripture tells us that God is like a father—well, I know some young people whose fathers aren't in any way providing a positive image of what a father is. I also know some strong, quiet men who are really conveying to their children the ideal father in a very adequate way.

As you discuss this, ask yourselves—have we possibly abrogated our Christian responsibility as parents to professionals? We've given the authority for education over to the schools, and, to a great degree, Christian education over to the church. Pictures in printed lessons won't take the place of a father. He can give up his authority for a short period of time on Sunday morning, but he can't give over his responsibility. This is the way you should present this matter to your husband.

My Husband Doesn't Spend Enough Time with the Children . . .

Our family lives in the suburbs of a large city. My husband spends at least an hour each way driving to and from work. Needless to say, he doesn't have much time to spend with the children, especially in the evening when they have gone to bed. And he's often impatient with them. I realize he's tired after a day at work and fighting rush hour traffic. But I also think it is important for him to spend time with the kids—for their sake as well as his. How can I help him have time to relax while still spending time with the children?

This is a common problem today. I'd like to start my answer by suggesting to this wife that she examine her own attitude toward her husband and his work. Often behind this kind of question is a resentment on the part of the mother because she has to spend all day with the kids and the husband seems to be getting off easy. When he comes come at the end of the day, she thinks that the least he could do is accept some of the burden. Instead, he seems tired out, preoccupied, and doesn't want to spend time with the children.

This is the formula for bringing about stress in the family and problems with the children. When the mother harbors a hidden sense of resentment over the fact that she is a mother, that she is carrying more than her share of the load, trouble is brewing.

In your case, I would examine this attitude, and also your attitude toward your husband's work. Do you feel his work is actually worthwhile, that what he's doing is something that needs doing? Do you really appreciate that fact that he actually is tired? We need to make peace with ourselves, to realize these are two callings we have—the husband to be the bread-winner and the wife to be the mother. Then we will be ready to talk about a little more harmonious situation.

When your husband comes home from work, give him some time to relax before you hit him with the problems of the day. Learn a little about his cycle—what does he need? Give him a chance to change his clothes and unwind before you start telling him which faucet is dripping, what window was broken, who was called into the principal's office, and the unexpected meeting he has to attend that evening. Let him sort of regroup himself—get his cells operating as a father, as opposed to driver and businessman. Give him time.

Then begin to plan ahead for things you can do with the kids. You can get a lot of mileage with children by saying, "A week from next Saturday, we're going to grandma's." Well, for two weeks then, you have them anticipating something and they feel they are getting dad's attention. Make sure you keep these appointments when you make them. But by planning ahead and letting him get psychologically prepared, you can spend more time with the children. If you give him a chance to unwind a little, you might find him a little less impatient.

My Husband Isn't Doing His Share . . .

My husband and I recently decided I should go to work. He was to help with the housework. Well, it started out great—he helped with the dishes, even the shopping. But the uniqueness of his new role has worn off. Now he has stopped lending a hand unless I bug him about it. What should I do? Should I stop asking him and do it myself, or continue to prod and poke, and risk becoming a nagging wife?

When you inaugurated this arrangement, you *both* decided that you should start to work. Now he's voted by himself to quit half the work. That is a rather uneven arrangement. You both decided, either for economic reasons, or because you wanted some role outside the home, that you should go to work. Now he has decided he'll renege on his part of the deal. You should both vote, rather than just one. Fair is fair. I think you need to face him with that. Simply tell him you could return to your former state (you do the housework and he goes out to earn a living).

Perhaps you really do not need more income. Maybe what you need to do is to recognize that you like a more traditional type of marriage. He likes to have you keeping the home and waiting on him hand and foot. Maybe you need to return to that arrangement because obviously he doesn't want to keep his part of the bargain.

There is another solution to this. Perhaps your husband doesn't feel like getting involved in household tasks at the end of the day (though I've met many men who find home chores quite challenging). One solution might be to bring in help from the outside. Use some of the additional income resulting from your work. By the way they discuss it, some people make household chores very demeaning. I don't share that. I think housework is a noble task. It is hard work. Because it is, you probably don't have the energy to work both in and out of the home.

So I'd suggest first: confront your husband with the idea that your initial decision was entered into unwisely. Maybe you should become a housewife again and live on less. On the other hand, if you do indeed need the double income, then he must pick up his share of the housework. If he doesn't feel he can pick up his half, I suggest that you bring in outside help and equalize the whole business. Right now it is too hard on you and eventually would put an unnecessary strain on your marriage. Talk with your husband and help him to see the unfairness of the present situation.

There Just Isn't Enough Money to Go Around . . .

Ever since I quit work to have a baby, we've had trouble getting along financially. We're not big spenders, and we do a pretty good job of sticking to a budget, but there just isn't enough money to go around. My husband says the only solution is for me to go back to work. I really dread the thought of it—not that I dislike work, but I've always felt it was important for a mother to raise her own child and not pawn the responsibility and enjoyment off on grandma or a hired baby-sitter. Do you have any suggestions?

So, your husband has decided the only solution is for you to go back to work? I'd like to spend some time on that statement—as to whether or not this is the only solution. Interestingly enough, Jesus says, "Which of you, intending to build a tower, sitteth not down first and counteth the cost?" (Luke 14:28). I think without doing this passage too much violence, one could say, "Which of you, intending to build a family, sitteth not down first, and counteth the cost?"

Costs are very interesting. Often there is an emotional cost —a woman has prepared for a certain occupation and is fulfilled by that occupation. All at once she finds herself with one of the aspects of the family—a child—so she says, "Can I do this thing that fulfills me psychologically, and still be a mother?"

It would be informative for you and your husband to sit down over this statement and attack it from two viewpoints. For one, add up how much you'd gain by going to work. By the time you bought new clothes, paid for transportation and a babysitter, faced the emotional strain, what would you gain? Add all that together and find out if the job you are contemplating is really going to cover those costs.

Then I'd suggest you take a look at your present budget again. There is an old adage that says, "Expenses rise to meet income." It might be helpful to go through your budget and ask, "How much are we spending that we don't need to spend?" Would it be less pain to do away with some things than face the pain of going to work? Try to bring those two things together.

If that doesn't do it, let me suggest another possible solution. Consider caring for another child in your home. Maybe taking care of two babies would be less struggle than going to work and leaving your baby with a sitter. Or perhaps there are other kinds of work you can get in the home—typing, telephoning, and so on. Would it be possible for you to get a part–time job in the evening when your husband would be home to watch your child?

These are possible alternatives. I tend to side with you in this particular situation. If at all possible, if there is a way, I'd suggest you take the responsibility of staying in the home when your child is so very young. When he goes to school and you have free time, that's another matter.

I Want to Pursue My Career . . .

I have two children, one in school and a three–year–old. I feel they need their mom at home, but lately I've been feeling worthless being just a homemaker. I was a teacher and all my friends have careers. I don't want to turn my children over to a babysitter, but I also feel guilty about not pursuing my career. How can I handle my feelings?

In our church we've come up with a motto which I think has value. That is, we've been learning to say to each other, "There is no such thing as a just–a." Society has ranked people like a boy scout troop. We have the eagle scouts, and then we work our way down to the tenderfeet. People say to me things like—I'm just a homemaker—just a plumber—just a carpenter—or just a principal. Just–a this, or just–a that. As if the only thing that would be worth doing would be President of the United States. I suppose then you'd say, I'm just President of the United States, and not God!

Very often young women say to me, "I'm just a mother." I ask, "What do you mean just a mother? That's the most important thing you can be, isn't it?" One of the great cries of the world is for people to care for their children. I'd suggest that you read Romans 12 to help you with this. Paul makes it clear that there is no such thing as a just–a. The Bible puts an argument together that says we are all parts of one body.

A daughter will say to her father, "I want to go away to college." Her father doesn't altogether understand college. He thinks it is just a place where you prepare for a trade or profession. His daughter is going to be a mother and a homemaker, so why does she need this? It costs so much to send her to school. So he'll say, "Well, you're just going to go away to college and waste my money. You'll spend $4,000.00 a year, and then you'll get married."

A few years later as she gets into her third year of college, sure enough she falls in love with some young man. Even though she's almost finished with her degree in nursing, she tells her father she wants to get married. He gets that "I told you so" look on his face. Then she says she will finish her degree. So she does, and then she gets married. Later she gets pregnant. Then every day she's saying, "Somehow I've got to show my father he was wrong—he didn't waste his money paying for my college education. I've got to go out and prove my worth by doing this thing I told him I would do."

Now is when you should bring the family together and say, "Hey, wait a minute—we all have value." The purpose of college wasn't necessarily to learn a certain trade; it was to become a certain type of person. Look what a wonderful thing has happened. I went to college; I met this man—what father wouldn't pay $10,000.00 for his daughter to meet the right man? Of course he would. So wait to have the outside career. Wait until some day when your children have grown. In the meantime you have value because you are a homemaker. There's no such thing as a just–a!

My Wife Wants to Go to Work . . .

My wife wants to take on additional responsibilities of some sort. It's true that she's not busy—she seems to have her house in shape an hour before breakfast, but I've seen what has happened in some other homes, where the wives became involved in extensive volunteer work, or found a part–time job, or started learning a new career. I don't want that to happen to my wife. But I don't want to hold her back either.

In a way I think you tip your hand by saying you're willing to go along. You seem to be the kind of person who is looking for moderation. You're looking for a warning here that something bad can happen. Well, what does happen? I think you're saying that in some cases the woman becomes more interested in her work than in her husband. In some cases the house doesn't get cleaned anymore, the meals aren't ready on time, and so on. She begins to lose interest in our thing together—those are your concerns, it would seem.

We all know of situations where this sort of thing has happened. However, for a man to be so insecure that he's afraid of his wife achieving is really frightening, too. So you need to examine your own life. Are you frightened by your wife's achievement?

One of the basic needs of all persons, men and women, is to have meaning in life—to make a contribution to the world. When the children are gone from the home (or perhaps before there are children), stop to think about what goes on within that place called a house. The home is what happens in human dynamics within the structure. Inside that house during the daytime, it's a pretty long time. Anyone listening to soap operas all day has to develop some very serious problems! So it would seem to me that there is a way to meet your criterion of moderation and still meet your wife's need to make a valuable contribution to the world.

If you have enough money, then volunteer work surely would be a wonderful thing. There are so many things to do for the Lord—in Christian activity, in the church, the hospital, etc. I'd encourage you to get your own security straightened out and decide in your own mind, "I'd be proud to have my wife doing these things." And get a little confidence in your ability to find this medium ground.

Let's face it: almost everything you can point to in human activity if taken to excess becomes a sin. Almost everything. That's what sin is made of. Satan has no raw material. He's no creator. He didn't make anything. All he does is twist and pervert things and get things out of context. God is the Creator. Satan is the perverter. It is possible to pervert something as decent, fine, and good as the human drive to make a contribution and to serve mankind. Satan could push someone to the excess that he spends all his time at that, to the neglect of his own family. What we're concerned about here is moderation, not excess. I think you are on the right track when you say, "I'm willing to go along."

My Husband Is a Workaholic . . .

When my husband went into business for himself, I knew he would be busy, but it is now all out of proportion. He's never home. I might as well be a widow for all I see him. And he is practically a stranger to the children. The wife should come first, then the children, then making a living. How would you rate these three responsibilities? It seems he has them backwards. How can I get this across to him?

Let's start at the beginning. You mention he started a new business. There is a Bible verse that applies to this. Luke 14:28 says, "Which of you, intending to build a tower, sitteth not down first, and counteth the cost?" I'd say that applies to starting a business as well. Often when a couple begins a new venture like a business, they forget to sit down and count the costs. Sometimes they'll be undercapitalized and may be destined for failure from the beginning. But I'm thinking about the cost of a man's life, time, and so on.

Most worthwhile ventures in life involve certain kinds of sacrifices. If this pressure your husband is going through right now is a temporary condition because he has just started the business (he probably doesn't have enough help, or isn't completely organized), he needs extra time to make it happen. It is unfortunate that this testing is taking place at a time when your children are growing up and you are feeling the tension. But you have to sit down first and realize that these are costs. I don't think your husband is doing these things because he wants to be an irresponsible husband! He's probably not thinking he will bring about an unhealthy family situation by just staying at work too long. He's trying to survive, so he has his own set of problems. Try to empathize with him and don't put him in the bad guy category. This is a situation you must confront together, and you have to find a way around it.

The Air Force did a study a few years ago concerning why certain Air Force children go bad and why certain Air Force children seem to be happy. It relates mostly to how the mother in the marriage feels about her husband's work. Is she always complaining? If she is, the children tend to grow up hating the Air Force, and they often rebel against their parents. Your attitude during this time is probably as important as anything going on. I suggest that you support your husband rather than criticize him.

You ask how I feel about your list of priorities. I tend to think this falls into a biblical pattern as well. First of all, a man's responsibility according to the Bible is to God. His second responsibility is to his family (and here I believe the wife should have priority over the children). There needs to be an intimacy between them even the children don't enjoy. Then I would list his friends, his community, his Christian brothers. I would put making a living last. These areas don't exist in a man's life like a train—one behind the other. They exist together, really, in a living, on–going situation. When you have to make choices one over the other, list them in this priority.

We Are Thinking of Starting a Family . . .

My wife and I are thinking of starting a family. Frankly, the thought of being a father frightens me. My father's example wasn't very positive. Neglect and abuse come to mind when I think of fatherhood. I certainly wouldn't want to be like him, but I have no idea how much discipline or affection should be shown. I must admit I even have a hard time thinking of God as my Father because of such negative experiences. My wife has been very understanding so far, but I want to get the problem resolved before we have children. What would help to erase the scars of the past so I can view God more fully and anticipate a family?

In most marriages people want to get things settled ahead of time (i.e., we'd like to get all the money in the bank so we'd be economically stable before we marry). We would like to have all the information about human and sexual relationships before we marry. Or we'd like to be mature enough—know all about human confrontation, how to solve problems, and so on.

I think the shared experience of most people is that marriage is not something you can prepare for in the same way you prepare for a final exam. It's not something you can cram for. Have you ever tried to save up sleep when you had a demanding week ahead? Sleep is something you just can't save up! It doesn't work that way. You have to get it in process. Experience at fatherhood is the same kind of thing. You have to pick it up in the process of being a father—you can't prepare for it totally ahead of time. To be sure, God has prepared us to a certain extent. He protects us in some ways biologically, and He can make us emotionally mature enough to handle fatherhood before we experience it. On the other hand, our culture has complicated family life so that men are biologically ready to be fathers before they are emotionally, spiritually, and economically ready.

But you are married and obviously a mature person—mature enough to be thinking and reflecting upon these problems. You've taken a giant first step. There are many people who become fathers just by happenstance and don't give it any thought at all.

Since you are concerned and have given thought to the matter, I'd suggest you go to some person or family whom you respect. Ask someone you consider to be a competent father about it. Observe how he handles his children. I think you'll find that to be a worthwhile step. You will learn later on that your youngest child had a better father than your older child. With each child you learn something.

Spend some time also forgiving your own father—I sense a real need here—especially since you have trouble picturing God as a father. Even though your own father may have been inept and perhaps even cruel, forgive him for the sake of your own soul as well as his. This will give you additional help at being a good father. You may need the forgiveness of your own children some day!

Should We Adopt a Child?

My wife and I have been married for three years and haven't been able to have children. The doctors can't tell us exactly what the problem is. It seems hopeless. We've talked about adopting children, but this has raised a question in our minds. Is it possible God doesn't want us to have children? Would adopting be against His will for us? We've talked to several Christian friends and received various opinions. My wife suggested I write to you. We'd hate to go against God's will, but we always did want to have a family. Can we know His will in this situation?

Yes, I suppose it is possible God may not want you to have children—but the question you really want to ask is, "Does He want us to or does He not want us to?" I partially reject the logic that says that we find out God's will by circumstances. If I believed the physical problem that you can't have children was God's voice speaking to you, then I would argue further that interference with any circumstance is against God's will. We ought to expect that every circumstance is God speaking to us. If we happen to get a disease we should accept it. The world is full of injustice, this is God speaking, and so on. I don't think that's the way it is. Now we don't have time here to find the total answer to this dilemma, but I'm confident God doesn't work that way.

You might ask yourself this question, first of all: Why not adopt a child? Are you and your wife in love with one another? Do you have the kind of marriage and home into which a child should come? The adoption agency with whom you deal will help you analyze this. They will give you psychological tests to tell whether you would be proper parents. Positive test answers would be another good indication as to whether you should adopt children or not. If all people were given psychological tests before they had children, the world probably would be a better place.

Does your vocation interfere with your ability to raise children? If you are both career people and both of you are interested above all in pursuing individual careers, then perhaps a child wouldn't be a welcome guest in your home.

Assuming that your answers to the above questions are positive—yes, you love each other. Yes, your home would be a good place to bring up a child. Assume that the psychological tests prove you are the kind of people who can handle parenthood. Assume that your vocation would not interfere, that you want children. Then, by all means, you ought to have them!

It appears to me that you are the kind of people who could raise a healthy child, emotionally, physically, spiritually. You could take one who has been rejected by society—through an involuntary thing like the death of his parents, or being an unwanted child, or an illegitimate child. Such children are full of insecurities and fears. When they come into a home full of love and the Spirit of Jesus Christ, think what a wonderful mission yours would be. I'd encourage you to pray along this line, and reject the logic that says God is speaking to you only through circumstances. If you push that fatalistic philosophy to its ultimate end, what a cruel world this would be!

Should We Bring a Child into This World?

Joan and I are both twenty-three and have been married for two years. Now we're settled enough to begin a family but a question has come up. Both she and I were raised in Christian homes and came to the Lord in our teens. But Joan's brother (raised in the same situation as she) has turned his back on all his religious and moral upbringing. That has shaken both of us badly. How can we be sure our children won't do the same thing? No matter how hard we try to be Christlike, there are so many bad influences in this world, from the kids next door to the kids in school, even the people in the church. It is a frightening thing to decide to bring a child into all of this. How can we justify such an awesome decision?

That awesome decision is the very decision God made when He decided on the human project to begin with. You ask how you can be sure your children won't do the same thing. Because of the nature of man, you can't be sure. One could ask your question in this way from God's point of view. Should I even start the human race? After having started the human race, some will indeed rebel against Me and will by necessity be separated from Me and be lost eternally. Therefore, to insure that there's no loss, we won't have the human race at all! When we bring children into the world, we need to understand that our risk as parents is much the same risk God took when He created the human race. His willingness to enter into this venture, in spite of the risks, should give us courage to go into this same venture ourselves.

There are some positive aspects about this matter as well. First, historically there have always been temptations in the world. For instance, would you have liked to have raised your child in the Roman world? What terrible perversions—what evil leaders! Children could see things on the street—immorality of any unimaginable nature. And yet many people grew up cleanly in those environments. So we bring our children into today's troubled world. Is our day more troubled than those days?

Keep this truth in mind: Your children not only run the risks connected with life, but they also have the privilege and responsibility of being the salt of the earth.

We can raise our children to understand the world is full of evil, but we have a chance to be good—to be God's people on earth—the chosen people. And we can bring our children up with this consciousness: we are here to make a difference —not to *absorb* our environment but to *affect* our environment for God.

Take the same leap of faith God has taken! With confidence and courage raise your family; love them as God is loving you. And as you love them, trust the Lord that they will be able to become an influence in this world to bring people to Jesus. Read 1 John 4:4, "Greater is he that is in you than he that is in the world."

What's So Bad about Not Having Children?

We've been married for six years and don't have any children yet, which is just the way we want it. However, people won't leave us alone. "Hey, you guys look like the all–American couple," they'll say. "How long you gonna wait?" Sometimes it's a joke—sometimes serious. Anyway, my wife and I are getting a little bit bugged about it. Right now we don't know for sure that we do want children—we don't know if we're ready for it. Frankly, we're getting tired of people always putting pressure on us. What's so bad about being married six years and not having any children? Also, how do we silence our church friends who are constantly badgering us?

I think this letter really speaks to the bankruptcy of our conversation with one another. I doubt whether most of the people really care whether you have children or not. They're probably coming up to you at church wanting to say something friendly or show some interest in you. The only thing they know about you is that you don't have children. So they say, "When are you going to have children?" The way to handle this situation is with a serious answer. Respond with: "Are you really interested in an answer to that question?" They'll probably be taken aback. Assuming that they are interested, then tell them how you feel—that you don't feel ready to have children. Tell them you don't feel you have to have children to make your lives complete. Or maybe you feel your occupation demands so much of you it would be unfair to have children. I think this approach will handle most of your problem.

People are just trying to find something to say. And isn't that great? They do want to talk to you. They want to say something. Perhaps it might be a good idea to raise this question in a Sunday school class sometime—the responsibility of having children. There are many people who do have children who probably shouldn't have had them—they didn't think it through very well. There's another side to the question that says, "God in his foreknowledge allowed nine months for pregnancy." In a sense, that nine months does more to prepare the prospective parents than to prepare the child for the world. The God I worship could cause the whole process to be speeded up to nine minutes if He wanted to. But He's doing it in nine months, partially to help us parents get ready, to prepare us emotionally and psychologically for this tremendous event.

You might find that your own lives would change greatly if you have children. Also think about your old age—do you want the freedom you have now to last forever? What about when you are old? Now you're saying, "Jay's coming at me, too, saying we ought to have children." No, I'm just urging you to think it through. When you're old you might not want as much solitude and freedom as you now seek. You must make these decisions early in life. This is the way I would answer your question.

Parent/Child Relationships:
Part Two.
Parents Are People, Too

My Son Knows Everything . . .

My son is driving me nuts. He acts like he knows everything. When I'm driving the car, he tells me everything I'm doing wrong. When we talk about politics he disagrees with my views. He doesn't agree with the local newspaper, and he accuses it of being prejudiced. Bring up any subject and he says, "Dad, things are different today than they used to be." He's turning into a regular smart aleck.

Your letter reminds me of a story. A man walked across a college campus. To the first student he encountered he said, "Good morning." And the student replied, "In relation to what?" Your son is going through a stage in life—an age when young people question anything and everything. There is something deeper here, however. Your son wants to play "king of the hill" with you. But criticizing your driving is something else. Just talking about politics and the local newspaper is one thing. Apparently he feels you need humbling, and he's going to find some way to do it. Have you implied to your son by your general attitude that you think you are always right—and he must be always wrong? Must you have the last word in everything? In that case he may be saying, "Dad is smart, and he knows a lot of things. But there must be a crack somewhere in his armor—I think I'll poke around until I find it. I'll find some weakness."

Maybe you can lower the pressure in this particular area by admitting up front that you don't have the answer to everything. Admit there are certain things you can learn about. Simply say, "Here's my view, and here's what it is based on."

The "generation gap" also enters the picture. If there is a chasm between father and son, it is probably over the why question. Young people are taught in today's educational system to question everything. They are not necessarily in the business of finding discreet information and trying to store it as we did a couple of generations ago. But they are encouraged to question everything. When a boy asks why today, or questions authority, it may not be because he wants to be a smart aleck. It may be just because he feels that all truths can stand up to questioning—and he wants to know the answer. He does understand something about the manipulation and maneuvering of information and truth—he is interested in getting behind it all and finding out why you believe what you believe.

Rather than just making flat statements to your son, perhaps it would be good to say, "Let me share my opinion—here's what I feel, and here are the reasons why I feel it." Then you might find out he'll be less anxious to fight about it. He may feel the things you believe aren't based on any logic at all. What he's really interested in is helping you to find a foundation for what he thinks may just be arbitrary statements. Maybe he thinks you have a naive approach to life. I seriously doubt that your approach is quite as naïve as your son thinks it is. Why don't you explore these areas with him?

How Can I Keep My Children from Watching TV?

Is there a sensitive way to keep my children from watching TV? With the R–rated movies popping up in droves, and regular TV hitting an all–time low on the moral scale, I just don't want them watching the set anymore. Not to mention the commercials. Any suggestions?

I have many suggestions, but they have to fit the individual home. First, go over the TV guide together at the beginning of the week. Make some selections. Decide how many hours you feel you ought to watch TV during the week, and make some definite decisions about it. Do your children want to watch a certain program? Help them decide which program to watch. The ratings and reviews are very helpful. In our guide we have a 2-, 3-, 4-star system on movies. There are very fine reviews written by local people. It takes a little time, but it's worth it. This practice saves you time—you don't have to watch some worthless thing. I surely would not want my children watching something the secular TV people didn't recommend for children.

No matter how careful you are, certain problems sneak through—commercials, for instance. I'm wondering just how far they will go in putting the intimate parts of our lives on TV! I'm amazed at the products openly advertised. When those awkward silences occur in our home, when embarrassing commercials are shown, I ask the children what is embarrassing. These are really good opportunities to talk about important subjects. If you don't talk about these matters, the kids think mom and dad are afraid to discuss them—or are ignorant. I want my children to know I'm not afraid of these things—or ignorant.

Certain matters are objectionable to me: I reject adultery, drunkenness, and many of the activities pictured on TV. Discussions of these matters are some of the best Christian educational opportunities we have in our home. They provide an opportunity to tell our children about Christian values, to show how Christian people can live in a very real world. I hope these suggestions will help you and generate other useful ideas.

How Can We Control What Our Children See on TV?

My wife and I are very selective in what we allow our children to watch on television. It has taken time, but we've come up with quite a few programs we think the kids can watch without being unduly exposed to violence. However, the stations in our area show previews of late night programming that are unfit for adults, let alone kids. Sometimes these previews come on during the shows we allow the kids to watch. Some of the commercials during these shows are pretty sensuous, too. When our local theater showed a preview of X—rated movies during G—rated films, a group of us protested and the manager changed his policy. TV is different. How can we get to the root of this problem?

I'm not sure TV is that different. In the case of your local theater manager, he simply responded to the economic facts of life—he didn't want people boycotting his theater, so he changed his policy. I'm confident that if people would speak up to the TV networks, we could make much progress there as well. In fact, some progress has been made. The attempt at family hour programming, for instance, has been quite successful. I realize the late night TV people poke fun at it, and they all seem to think it is a big joke. By and large, these critics are people who are going through their third or fourth marriages. Their children are involved in things you and I wouldn't approve. Their values are different. So I don't take that kind of criticism too seriously.

We can say what we feel—write letters to the networks and express our opinions. These people are very concerned about the marketplace, so they will respond.

Then look at the problem from another perspective. I wonder sometimes why we have a TV in our home. It would be a relatively simple matter to get rid of the thing. TV has a place of prominence or nonprominence in the home largely based on the way people view it—as being central or not central. How creative are we in the use of our time? How many things do we do together? TV can either dominate us or we can use it as a helpful tool. When these questionable things come on, when you see something evil (violence, sensuality, and so on) and your children are sitting there watching, then is the time to stop and discuss it. You cannot hide your kids in a closet —you can't keep them from these things. They hear and see things in school (behavior, language, activities) that are appalling. You must stop and examine these things. What is evil about them? Why is God opposed to them? When they see the whole picture and understand we're really concerned about protecting them, that they might enjoy life to its fullest, then they will begin to participate with us in the reasoning process. They will have their own built-in censor to help them cope with life's realities.

My Son Is a TV Addict . . .

What do you do with a son who is just plain lazy? He comes home from school and just flops in front of the TV. His mother can't get him to do a thing at home, and neither can I. We've tried all sorts of things. He doesn't have any hobbies. It just seems he's bored with life. What can I do to make him wake up a little?

This is a challenging problem—and a common one! Some of you readers may think it sounds strange, and some may say, "Hey, that's my boy!" It reminds me of a young man at a conference. He was about 17. After I spoke, he said, "I have something to get settled with the Lord. I've been asleep for five years! I've been watching TV steadily from the time I come home from school until I go to bed. I'm hooked on the thing. It's like I'm Rip Van Winkle. And all at once as a result of your message tonight, I realized I've been wasting the life God gave me, and now I've got to do something about it." We sat down and prayed. I opened the Word of God and showed him how to commit his life to Christ. Then he decided he just wanted to make his life count from that point on.

Later, we met together and tried to probe this. How did he

get into it? He said that in his case, he became unable to cope with the world around him. He found TV a way to slip into never-never land, and he compared it to a tape deck. It was as if someone took a tape and plugged it into him. The tape would just run him every day. That's the way he was on TV. It wasn't just laziness, but he was actually unable to cope with the world around him.

In your letter you say you've tried many things. I'd like to suggest a couple more. Your son needs to have his reward tied to some effort. I don't think an allowance is something a son has coming just because he's born into a family. So one motivation might be economic. Insist that he do certain things to get him out of that chair to earn an allowance. Make that a strong point.

Then get him involved in something outside the home—a stress camp or bicycle trip. This would tie the reward to expending some energy with some achieved goal. There are many boys like your son. But with some of them it's astounding: get them on a bicycle; face them with a challenge. Perhaps they're used to quitting when they get tired, but if the rest of the boys keep riding and he's left there, that's pretty lonely. This approach also might "wake him up a little." Make this a matter of prayer and the Lord will show you the approach to take.

What about Homework?

Our twelve-year-old daughter comes home from school about 3:30 in the afternoon and plays until supper. When we ask her about homework, she says she has very little. She doodles with it after supper so that she is always pleading to stay up later than she should. She gets very upset when she isn't able to finish it, because she feels the teacher will lower her grade. We don't like to see her sleeping time cut down. How can we best motivate her either to start her homework earlier, or to do it more quickly?

You sound like my wife with this letter! This struggle goes on in most homes— and I'm not sure this is a battle we ever win. You just continue to fight! One of the characteristics of the adolescent child is that he tends to put things off. He also has a shorter attention span. So it is the very nature of adolescence to have this problem.

A friend told me that in his family a child does not have supper until he finishes his homework. This might be a good idea in your case, since your daughter comes home early. On the other hand, I sympathize with children in this situation. They've been in school all day, nose to the grindstone, as it were. Some would need an hour or so of play (and maybe even vigorous play) between school and settling down to do homework.

But life is real; life involves accepting responsibility. You can't live without it—it's simply the way it is. Many young people think they can avoid responsibility. I don't want to be in the group who thinks, *That's the trouble with youth today*. Youth today is like youth yesterday—they need the same values and they ought to be getting them from their parents. One of these values is learning to accept responsibility.

In college I belonged to a fraternity. I was nineteen at the time. The older men in the fraternity had the idea that pledges to that fraternity should do well in their studies, so they had study tables. We were forced to sit there many hours a day whether we wanted to or not. These men knew what adolescence was all about—they were barely out of it themselves.

The same is true in a home. Children should be encouraged to sit down and work on their homework even when they say they don't have any (they usually do!). What they're really saying is that they want to put it off. All of us have been in school. We know the problem of procrastination. That turns your little difficulties into one horrendous problem!

I am not opposed to staying up all night with a child to get something done. I remember sitting up with one of our children until 5 A.M. working on a paper. I drank coffee and he cried, but he stayed at it. By morning we could say, "Wouldn't it have been better if we could have done it in small steps rather than all at once?" With that particular child we seem to have conveyed the message. So stay at it—you'll win the battle about the time they leave home! But this is part of being a parent. Why didn't they tell us this at the altar?

I'm Concerned About My Neighbor's Children . . .

My neighbor and I are close friends. She listens to your program and respects your opinion, so maybe your advice on this matter would be helpful. She has four children—eighteen, sixteen, thirteen, and eleven. The eleven-year-old is picked on so much by the other three that he has developed quite an inferiority complex. His grades are poor and he isn't as good-looking or socially accepted as the others either. My neighbor tries to encourage her child, but she doesn't realize how much teasing he's getting from the older three behind her back. Is there any way to break the older children of their bad habit and salvage some self-respect for this little guy?

I don't know. Many eleven-year-olds have grown up with this same kind of problem. They seem to have survived. Children can be very cruel. Strangely enough, they are often most cruel to their own brothers and sisters. Sometimes this comes from jealousy and resentment of the younger child—"he gets all the breaks."

You mention being close friends with your neighbor. Let me suggest we look at this business of close friends just a bit. As close friends you probably talk about important things, not just the weather and routine matters. David Augsburger has a helpful book on this subject called *Caring Enough to Confront*. He talks about the Christian grace of being able to go to a person as a friend in Christ. Such friends can talk honestly about problems. Sit down with your friend and simply say, "Here's something I've been observing. Obviously, I don't live in your home. I don't see what's going on all the time. But from where I'm sitting, here's what I'm seeing." Now meddling is involving yourself in someone else's life. You really don't love them or care. You aren't willing to admit that you may be wrong. But caring enough to go to your neighbor and say, "I've been watching this situation, and this is what I see," is not meddling.

It may be that you ought to sit down with the older children and ask them if they are aware of what they are doing to their brother. As a Christian friend and a neighbor, simply share with them the seriousness of this. Occasionally when you try to do something like this, it will backfire on you. The other person may resent it and say it is none of your business. But usually people are looking for friends who care enough to help them with their problems. Too many just sit off on the fringe and cluck their tongues, wringing their hands, saying how awful it is. An objective neighbor who cares would be a great help in this situation. I'd start by talking to your friend and then to the older children. Let them know what they're doing.

Our Children Don't Want to Move . . .

Last month my husband was promoted to regional director in his electronics company. There had been nine other applicants for the job, and we were very pleased at his success. However, this change means moving from the general office to a location eighty miles away. When we told the children we were moving to another city, they were disappointed and complained that they would be leaving all their old friends behind. That was a week ago. Since then they have been brooding and won't speak to either my husband or me. We've discussed the whole thing together and frankly are considering passing up this whole promotion. Yet this is something my husband has been working toward for years. I know he'll be very hurt if we decide not to move.

This problem is more and more prevalent in our culture. Industry does demand mobility. Statistics tell us that in families with fathers under forty years old, the typical family moves every three years. This can be very upsetting to children. They become adjusted to one group of friends and one situation, and then they are uprooted. When this happens, the children often find themselves withdrawn. They are afraid to really get involved in new friendships, developing a new life in a new place.

I'm concerned about your children's response to this situation, the fact that they won't speak to you or your husband. If you respond to this behavior, in a sense you are honoring it. That is, if they find they can get their own way by using the silent treatment, or punish you for a situation larger than yourself, you'll be putting yourself in quite a trap. By honoring this attitude you reinforce negative types of behavior.

I'm opposed to a family ever responding to this kind of pressure. I respond to children when they are happy, rational, and open. When they are negative, it turns out to be a waiting game. I wait until they are out of it so we can talk about it rationally.

In this situation I suggest you tell the children you are ready to talk about it when they are. Then, when you have come to that time, I'd put before them the fact that this must be a family decision. It does involve all of you. Dad isn't just someone out there bringing home the bacon—he is a person. He's built his own life around heading in certain directions within his occupation. The children should face up to his aspirations, needs, and desires—as well as their own. Your children at the ages of eleven and thirteen are at a time in life when it is probably easier for them to move than at some other period. Your daughter at eleven is just ready to go into junior high. Your son is ready to go into high school. It is a good time for a transition. I'd suggest that you sit down and discuss this adjustment. Help them to see it's not just their needs to consider, but dad's as well. This will open up the situation, and then you can make a better decision.

My Daughter Ties Up the Phone . . .

We have a phone and two extensions in our home, but we might as well not have any. My daughter ties up the phone every day after school and all weekend long. Should I do what my neighbor did and get my daughter a separate phone? If I don't, I may never make another phone call after 4 P.M.!

Most homes with teen-agers have this problem! Yours is a typical situation. For many, the idea of a separate line is absolutely unthinkable for economic reasons. For others, however, it's something they've already done. This is one way to solve the problem. Sometimes the young person pays for the phone out of his allowance, and sometimes the parents do it as an indulgence. However, I don't like to see this particular problem solved in a purely economic way.

There is really a deeper situation here. It has to do with citizenship and living together. A college president or dean would tell us something they discovered quite early—which young people learned to live in a home as good citizens, and which ones didn't. They know the ones who had everything their own way, who listened to the radio whenever they wanted to, who went out as they pleased. Some students type when others are trying to sleep, and do other inconsiderate things.

Young people divide into two categories. One group understands consideration for others, and the other does not. Telephone usage is a good way to begin to teach consideration for others. There are other people living in the home as well, and we need to begin to impress this on our children. Even if you didn't want to make calls after 4 P.M., is it fair to the other families whom your daughter is calling? What about the other girl's father? What does he think about all this?

There is a need for time limits, a time to say, "Can you stop this conversation in a moment or two?" Don't just say, "Stop now." Give your daughter a chance to wind it up. Set some rules for the phone, and your children will learn to use the rules. Some people put an egg timer by the phone, and when they start a conversation, they turn it over. Why should one hang up the phone? You want to show consideration. Someone else may want to use it. You control yourself. Your daughter will learn to control that internal meter—out of respect for others.

Once you learn to operate this way on the telephone, the same consideration will operate in all other areas of life. The Bible says: "In honor preferring one another." It's a good lesson to learn on the phone.

My Son Manipulates My Husband and Me . . .

My husband and I are being manipulated by a very clever teen-age son. The other day he came to me and asked permission to use the car for an hour before supper. I told him no, that he'd have to rake the leaves first. So he went down into the basement and approached my husband who was tinkering with an old TV. My son got a yes answer from my husband, so off he went in the car. It's not the first time he's played us off against each other. He's become very good at it. What do we do to head off this newly discovered talent?

Our country's early motto was, "United we stand, divided we fall." That's the way it must be in the family situation. As husband and wife, we sometimes inadvertently create a situation that results in this particular problem. A child comes to his father and asks a question. The parent is preoccupied and says, "Don't bother me. Go ask your mother." Through being shuttled back and forth from one parent unwilling to make a decision to another one, the child learns which parent is the soft touch and which one isn't. He learns that if he goes to one he gets a yes, and from the other he gets a no. It's a subtle kind of betrayal really—one parent becomes a good guy and the other a bad guy.

Young people will tell you this. Generally they know which subject bothers dad and which troubles mom. So there are some ways to deal with this. For one thing, I'd say that when your son comes up and asks if he can do a certain thing, ask him if he's talked to the other parent about it already. If he has, ask him, "What did he/she say?" "She said no." "Well, then, why are you talking to me?" In this way he will get the idea that there is no way he can divide and conquer. There's no way he can drive a wedge between you two.

There are times when you cannot be dogmatic. Rather than give a no, it's more fair to say you need to think about it. Don't always come back with a "no." That will make you the arbitrary parent, and your spouse the thoughtful parent. Sometimes the best answer is to say you need time. Then go behind a closed door. Talk it through with your spouse. If the other parent has made a decision, even what you feel is a poor one, stick with him. Be loyal to him in every way. In this situation, you'll lose more by raising questions or causing your child to think you are divided, than you'll gain by seeming to be more fair. "United we stand, divided we fall!"

Sometimes I Become Angry with My Children . . .

We have an extremely active four–year–old son and a quieter two–year–old daughter. In view of their differences, I often find it hard to know what is normal. Because of this, I've had a difficult time handling situations. I try to respond in love, but sometimes anger creeps in. Could you recommend a book on normal childhood behavior at various ages and how to handle problem situations? Our whole family would be helped by this. We've already received suggestions that have made changes for the better.

I'd suggest two authors—Bruce Narramore and James Dobson. Go to a Christian bookstore and look at the titles listed under those two men. You will find information very helpful to you. As to what is normal, that is a provocative question. Normal would be what happens when you toss all people into a hat and mix them together and come up with an average. There probably is no such thing as a normal person. What we have is two extremes—abnormal people at each end, and a range of behavior in between that we find acceptable. There are acceptable behavior patterns near each end of that range —more active or less active children who may be encountered within a typical family. And there are those who fall beyond those ranges. They cannot be controlled by any particular family.

You seem to have a typical situation—boys tend to be a little more boisterous than girls, a little more difficult to handle. That comes with the territory. Perhaps your medical doctor could help you a little with this problem. He could do some testing to see if your boy's hyperactivity is related to some sort of imbalance in his glandular makeup. In some cases certain medications or even natural foods can help control hyperactivity. I doubt that is your son's problem. There is a marked contrast between your children. You'd possibly like a combination of the two natures. But that isn't the way it works!

Bruce Narramore's book, *An Ounce of Prevention*, would be helpful to you in helping to deal with specific situations. It is a very practical study guide. Since your children are two and four this would be a great time to begin applying those principles. If you want your children to develop favorable behavior patterns, now is the time to get started!

My Grandson Is So Shy . . .

I'm terribly concerned about my grandson—he's extremely shy. I've never known him to initiate a conversation, and his mother seems to think he has very few friends at school. All he does is sit around the house and read books, mostly science fiction and mysteries. His guidance counselor at school says he gets excellent grades and ranks extremely high among the other students. But she is also concerned about his lack of relationship with other pupils. Does he need counseling?

Perhaps he does. I would suggest that a caring pastor, youth pastor, or Christian counselor might be able to help him with this—if the boy considers it a problem. It may be that you consider it a problem, and his mother may consider it a problem. But you have a preconceived idea about what makes a person socially competent—that is, sometimes salesmen feel the more you talk the more competent you are. Other people would feel it's not necessarily so. I've spent a little time with the American Indian community in the Southwest. There, among the young men, the more silent the better. They consider silence to be a virtue and talking to be pretty much a sign of weakness.

I don't want to treat your question with levity, but Charlie Jones talks about a boy who was so shy he couldn't lead in silent prayer. I guess that's about as shy as you can get. Let me suggest—some boys are just quiet and that's a good thing. Silence can be a valuable virtue. All of us need solitude and time alone—a quiet time. So don't worry about that aspect too much.

You say your grandson reads mostly science fiction and mysteries. Some would call this "escape literature." That may or may not be true in this case. Many young people who read mysteries and science fiction are really trying to learn about life. Science fiction usually takes a serious problem and tries to put it into a futuristic situation so as not to frighten us. This way we don't have to deal with it as a real issue.

Your grandson has a high IQ, you say—he's interested in reading. I would think that this boy will, when he feels a sense of confidence in the world, begin to come out of himself. He'll always be a quiet young man—and aren't you glad everyone doesn't chatter all the time?

I'd urge you not to worry so much about him. Pray for him and also trust that as he begins to learn more and more in his private life, he will take some risks out in public. He will begin to share some of his opinions with people and he will find a group of friends who like the kinds of things he likes. Then he will begin to come out of himself. This is usually the way it happens.

One further thought: sometimes a boy like this has an unrealistic perfectionism in his life. He is afraid to fail, so he ventures nothing for fear people will make fun of him. When you are talking to him, be sure you don't make fun of his ideas and thus make him draw back into his shell any further. Let time work its magic in his life—and let God do His part!

My Daughter Embarrassed Us . . .

My problem is our children when we have company. The other night we were entertaining my husband's boss, and I thought we had things pretty well under control. I had warned the children in advance to be on their good behavior; the meal was going great, and we were all listening to our guest talk about some of his projects. Then our seven–year–old asked for the rolls. We were listening so closely to the boss that no one heard her, so finally she yelled at the boss, in an irritated way, "Will you pass me the rolls?" My husband and I were embarrassed to tears. How can we handle these incidents?

This sounds like a comical scene. The reason it is funny to us is that all of us can identify with a situation like this. It has happened in almost all of our homes. I think specifically of a friend whose son picked up his cereal bowl and drank from it while a guest was there for breakfast. The father reprimanded him, but the son said, "Well, daddy, you do that." This happens in families.

To begin with, I really believe that this is why we should have guests in our homes. It's an opportunity to teach children certain behavior patterns. Let's face it: the boss was probably a little bit pompous, a little more interested in his own world than he should have been. When you set a child down at a table, he's part of the group. You're saying that by the seating arrangement. He feels he shouldn't be talked around, past, or through as if he weren't even there. So practice makes perfect and out of these mistakes come the lessons.

But back to your problem. It is embarrassing. I think more exposure, not less exposure, is what your children need. Many mothers feel that when this sort of thing happens, they shouldn't have people in their home—they'll be embarrassed. Go over the situation with the children, but don't get them too uptight. One of the reasons they become clumsy is over-emphasis on our part. We make too much of a situation, and they get so tense they make mistakes they normally wouldn't make. They're trying too hard to be on their good behavior. Take them out to restaurants, invite people over—friends who would understand this sort of thing.

We had a nice experience at our table the other day. A small boy was sitting with us, the son of a good friend of ours. The boy finished his meal ahead of the rest of us, so he asked for permission to leave the table. His father said, "No, we want you to hear what we're saying, and we want to hear what you're saying." That boy sat there for the whole meal! I was impressed. It was good experience for him to learn how to sit quietly and listen. I probably would have told him to go play with his trucks, but really it was a good lesson. We must practice in private the things we want to happen in public!

I Wish My Son Hadn't Talked to Our Pastor . . .

I don't think I've ever been so hurt in my life. My son told me last night that for some time now he's been talking to our pastor about his problems at home. In the first place, I didn't even know he had problems. I thought everything was going along just fine. So you'd think the least he could have done would be to come to me first. I don't know how I'm going to face our pastor now that he's heard what awful parents we are. I just don't understand this. After you go through so much trouble to raise your children, why do they do this to you?

You sound embarrassed—and that's a problem we can all understand. None of us want to be embarrassed—and none of us want to think we've failed. This is true of our whole Christian subculture (the evangelical subculture especially). We're so concerned that we might have a problem. If I were asked to point to any encouraging signs in the last two decades, or perhaps twenty–five years, I'd say it is our increasing acknowledgment as Christians that we can indeed have problems. Christians do have difficulties and they need to solve them as much as anyone else.

In a sense, the rain falls on the just and the unjust. The Christians have their problems and the world has its problems. So the fact that your family has some rough spots on its road doesn't mean you've failed in any sense of the word. It probably means your home is normal. It's just that you are coming out in to the open.

I'm quite confident your pastor has heard enough boys talk to weigh what boys say. When a boy tells me, "My parents don't love me," I'm not foolish enough to reply, "Oh, that is the kind of parents you have." That would indeed be unwise.

In fact, a young person will say to me, "My folks don't love me." And I'll reply, "Why do you feel that way?"

"Well, they're always picking on me. They always want me in at a certain time, and they want me to dress in a certain way."

"Why?"

"They don't want me to get in trouble."

"Why?"

"Oh, they're concerned about their reputation."

"Is that all they're concerned about?"

"No, they don't want me to get hurt."

"Why?"

"Well, I guess they love me."

That's often how it goes. If you have much to do with young people, you learn to take this sort of thing in stride. Probably your pastor is able to handle this well. One of the wonderful things about being a member of the local church is that we can have friends who will substitute for us when we're not there. I don't believe that young people are going to talk to their parents about everything. They'd rather talk to a caring adult, a teacher, scoutmaster, and so on. The apostle Paul tells us: "When I am weak, then am I strong." To a degree as we indicate our weakness and allow our Christian brothers and sisters to help us, we're really strengthening the whole body of Christ. It appears to me that this has happened to you. Probably in the future you will have opportunity to talk to your pastor. Then you can present your side of the story.

I'm Worried about My Son . . .

Lately my son has been running around with a rowdy bunch of boys in his high school. He came home smelling strongly of after–shave lotion—but I'm sure I also caught the smell of smoke. If he's smoking, which I'm quite sure he is, he's probably drinking, too. I'm worried about this, but I'm not sure how to go about stopping it. He'll probably deny it if I say anything. What can I do?

Most fathers don't want their children to smoke. In fact, most fathers who smoke don't want their sons to smoke. You'll probably think I'm always taking the young person's side (which I'm not) but let me note this: I caught a tone in your letter that bothers me just a little. "If he's smoking, he's probably drinking." I can understand your logic, but perhaps you are selling your son short. You have the idea that one thing follows another. Perhaps you're saying you never built any character into him, that he can't stand certain temptations. My guess is that he can. He's been raised in a good home. He should have quite a bit of character and personal strength.

Let's assume your son is caught up in the crowd. Think of your own teen–age years—wasn't it pretty important for you to be accepted by certain people? Perhaps these rowdy boys run the school. They are considered the in–group. Your boy somehow feels that acceptance by that group is important. Maybe he is bending his own morals just a bit to fit in with them. My feeling is, given enough time he'll begin to see the shallowness of these boys. As a result of all the teaching he's received (the Bible, Sunday school, good home life), he'll be able to see through some of these things.

I'd encourage you to have some faith in your boy. Sit down and talk with him—about the smoking habit, the fact that it is a health hazard. Emphasize that those little signs on the packs are put there for a reason. The ads haven't been taken off TV because it's a nice thing to do—cigarettes are still a health hazard. Point these things out to him.

Probably getting him into contact with different young people would help. Call your youth pastor and tell him your situation. Ask him to invite your son to some activities where he can be accepted by another group. I believe when he begins to compare the two kinds of people, he'll find himself wanting to be with the church group. It might work; it might not. In the meantime pray for him—and try very hard not to be too judgmental. Let God work in this situation.

My Daughter Complains about Rules . . .

My daughter is constantly complaining about the rules I make around home. I don't think it's too much for a parent to ask young people to come in on time, limit their social activities, watch how much they spend, and see that they devote time to their studies. I always hear the same argument, "Other parents don't have so many rules." I think the reason today's kids have no respect for authority is that people don't make enough rules and stick by them. What do you think?

I tend to agree with you. But I want to suggest something else to you. Suppose we are both right here? What does that prove? We both know it and agree. We feel we have the right track, and others are wrong—but the point is, what do we do about it? In this particular situation, how do you convince your own children to accept these rules? And what do you do about it when they say their other friends don't have rules?

Sometimes I feel there is a conspiracy called "others." Everyone uses the "others." I imagine your children's friends are saying to their parents, "My friends don't have any rules." Maybe the parents should get together to find out if this group called "others" really exists at all. I question whether it does in most communities. There may be no people who make rules and manage to keep them. That's quite possible. There may be parents in a typical high school who don't have much control over their children. It's usually true. But it's not as universally true as our kids want us to believe it is. Still, there are many desperate parents around who need help.

If you're saying the others in a church, that's an entirely different matter. The church is the crucial place for a Christian family as far as discipline is concerned. It's important for parents in the church to get together and talk about these things. They need to establish some rules and then back each other up on them. As I've said before, "United we stand—divided we fall!" Kids shouldn't be able to use one set of parents against another. Within the body of Christ in the church family, you can stand together. This will give you the example of some parents you can point to and say, "Wait a minute! Here are some people who feel a certain way."

Probably the PTA would be a good vehicle for this kind of action, too. There are times a Christian parent ought to bring an issue like this to the PTA and say, "Here's a problem we're facing . . . that group called the 'others,' who don't discipline." We have to be reasonable in our demands, however. I've seen community codes set up by parents alone. But when parents and children together determine the rules, they are usually more stringent than the parents had in mind in the first place. So try cooperation instead of competition.

My Daughters Are 'Women's Libbers' . . .

My three daughters are quite a trio. One is an eleventh–grader; one is in eighth grade; the third is a seventh–grader. It seems to me that ever since they were little they were on their way to being leaders in the women's lib movement. They have constantly challenged me with, "Daddy, that isn't fair," or "You make the rules too tough." Lately, and I know you're not going to believe this, they have been saying stuff like "That rule is discriminatory. We have our rights, too." Last week the three of them confronted me at the supper table and suggested that all rules in the future be decided by family conference. Now I respect their intelligence, but I feel that parents should make the rules. Who is right?

I don't know that I can tell you who is right, but I can tell you this. We have to face the fact that girls are being exposed to a great deal of education propaganda on the subject of women. This is the major social issue at the moment. The women's position is being discussed everywhere—and rightly so, in my opinion. A few generations ago, maybe two, if you had said women were going to vote across the world and take part in democracy, people would have laughed at you. Woman's position in the world has changed and we've come to terms with that. I doubt there's a man who would say women shouldn't vote.

There are certain other issues we men have ignored—or we have just been ignorant about them. But our little girls are learning about these matters. They're overreacting probably. The pendulum will swing too far, and we will see some foolish things. Then it will swing back to some central point. But things will be different with our daughters—let's face it.

As to your own family and making decisions and rules. I believe that generally speaking young people rebel against rules when they think they are arbitrary. They need to understand how these decisions were made. I think family conferences have tremendous value—but not for *changing* the rules.

In fact, I've learned that if you give young people the right to make rules, such as a community curfew, they will set tougher rules than a committee of parents would develop on the same subject. This is probably because they know some of the pitfalls. One of the values of the family conference is that it helps your children to see the logic by which you set rules. You are not just being arbitrary when you say to come in at a certain time. There are certain problems connected with staying out too late, going certain places, or doing certain things—and you know it. The conference can be an educational process for you—but it can be for your children as well.

My Husband Refuses to Discipline Our Children . . .

I'd like to know what a wife and mother is supposed to do when a husband refuses to discipline his children. We have one teen–age daughter and two sons seven and nine. When I get angry I threaten that their dad will punish them when he gets home. When he does comes home, he just says, "Say you're sorry, and promise not to do it again." I don't want to be the one to give out all the punishment. But my husband just won't do his share.

This appears to be an uneven situation. It must cause a great deal of anxiety for both you and your husband. First of all, you're asking your husband to support you in this matter of discipline—and we can understand that. Cooperation is very important in a marriage relationship.

On the other hand, from your husband's viewpoint, he's probably had a busy day. He's undoubtedly had various difficulties. No doubt he thinks of his home as a place to relax, a haven, a place where people love and respect him. All day long he's probably fighting for survival in his work. He may think of the family as a nest to come home to. Thus when he does come home to find the very first thing facing him is a discipline problem—he doesn't welcome it. To him it seems you are making him the grim reaper. You want him to come home and immediately administer discipline—to his beloved children, by the way, who he's probably been looking forward to seeing. Perhaps he's had a mental vision of hugs and kisses —and all at once he's robbed of that.

The two of you need to get your acts together—sit down and discuss what this really is all about. Perhaps the discipline is something that ought not to wait for dad's return. In any event, let dad relax first when he comes home. When he comes up the driveway, does the dog lay back his ears, put his tail between his legs, and run to the backyard? Do all the children huddle behind things waiting for their spanking? That isn't exactly what dad has in mind. So let him unwind a little.

Perhaps after the evening meal you can explain to him exactly what the situation was. Then perhaps the two of you should discipline the children together. Come up with something appropriate. One thing about discipline, often it is related more to how the person doing the disciplining feels than anything the child has done. Discipline must be commensurate with the infraction.

I also happen to believe there are few discipline situations that ought to wait until dad comes home. The time that elapses between the infraction and the discipline should be as brief as possible. Most of these situations should be handled by you, mother. On the other hand, I don't feel that you're being unreasonable in your major request here. Your husband must accept his responsibility. Just give him a chance to get it together before he has to assume the role of the disciplinarian.

Our Son Smokes . . .

Our son smokes. My husband and I worked out a plan to induce him to quit. We promised him if he'd stop smoking, we'd give him the down payment for a motorcycle. He agreed and he quit smoking, so we bought the motorcycle. And he immediately started smoking again. So we promised to make two payments on it if he stopped smoking again. He did until we had made those two payments. Then he started again. This has happened four times. He is still smoking and we've invested all that money for nothing. How can we get him to stop smoking?

There's an old saying that goes, "Fool me once, shame on you; fool me twice, shame on me." After four times, it seems to me your son is really taking advantage of you. Some time earlier in this boy's life he must have learned that there is no penalty for breaking promises, that you can continue to break promises and still get your own way. You just manipulate people. I'm much more concerned about your son's manipulative spirit than I am about his smoking. True, smoking is a national health problem. States are even passing laws about impairing the health of others by smoking in their presence.

In your case, however, you've traded one problem for two. You've traded a headache for an upset stomach. I think you ought to deal with the problem of not keeping promises first. I would impound the motorcycle until he's repaid the payments he owes. Thus he will learn you can't just use people. He will learn that you keep your word. The world is run by natural laws. Certain consequences follow as a result of our actions. Because we love our children, we must teach them that there are laws.

Really, this isn't too different from the smoking problem. That's one of the natural laws, too. If you fill your lungs with tar and vapors, this will cause cancer. It might also cause emphysema. Smoking will do things to you. But if a boy feels that a natural law doesn't operate, that you can break your promises and everything will turn out rosy, he has a problem. Maybe he does this to everyone he meets—he just keeps selfishly moving on his own way. So far he hasn't learned that there is a penalty. Start imposing the penalty right now. Get the payments before he goes back to riding the motorcycle. You will be doing him a favor. "Spare the rod, and spoil the child." He'll complain. But your son is sharp. He has shown he is resourceful. So make him use his resourcefulness in constructive ways. Stand firm, and above all, don't give in to him again!

My Children Are Rebellious . . .

My children are five, three, and the youngest is only sixteen months old. They have been a blessing, but they can be a hassle, too. Sometimes it is hard to believe how rebellious they are. I can't imagine what they'll be like when they become teen-agers. We have certainly not spared the rod, but spanking seems to have little lasting effect. I never thought I'd be writing to someone like you for advice, but you have made your expert opinions available, so why not? How can we be sure they won't totally turn against us in a few years? Is rebellion normal in kids this age?

Yes, rebellion is normal. Somehow the idea has crept into our culture that babies are wonderful, unspoiled, pristine individuals who become corrupted by the world. Really, it works the opposite way. I think babies come into the world with tremendously strong hostilities. If they have the right kind of environment, there is a civilizing effect from living in the world. Commitment to Jesus Christ is the ultimate civilizing effect, the purpose for which God created man. St. Augustine once commented that it is fortunate for mothers and parents that children are so uncoordinated. The truth is, if they were bigger, and better coordinated, when they throw their little temper tantrums, they would probably strangle their mothers! Watch a little child clenching his fists, throwing a tantrum in his crib. What if he weighed 200 pounds! That would be a frightening experience. Yes, I believe rebellion is normal in children this age.

Let me just lift another sentence from your letter—"writing to someone like me." Let's clarify something. Who am I? I'm simply a fellow pilgrim, another Christian attempting to work out my life in the light of the Bible and experience. Fortunately for me, I suppose, I've had many contacts with many families because of my work with Youth for Christ.

Beyond that—expert? Someone said, "X is the unknown quantity and spurt is a drip under pressure." I guess I would qualify on that basis. The truth is, I am, like all Christians, an individual who works out his relationship with God on a personal basis through Jesus Christ. I attempt to find answers that will help others. I'm not the answerman—I probably don't have as many answers as encouragement and help.

Children, when they are small, need discipline; they do need this physical training. I recommend two authors. I feel they really have much to offer the Christian world in this area of discipline and child training. James Dobson's *Dare to Discipline* and Bruce Narramore's *An Ounce of Prevention* deal with small children. These two men present ideas that are practical and biblical as well. Refer to them.

I Wonder If We're Strict Enough?

Everyone talks about a generation gap and all that, but I don't believe in it. I don't believe kids are any different now than when I was growing up. But they certainly are treated differently! They are treated like kings—they don't have to work, and they talk back to their parents. Don't you think if they were brought up properly, I mean by parents who were much stricter, that there wouldn't be so many problems?

I can certainly identify with this letter. We've all felt like this writer, I'm sure. You may be right. I don't know. Without question, there are problems in our youth culture today, just as there are in the adult world. We must do more than pinpoint the problems, however. We must look for answers. Now that you have these comments out of your system, and you've said what you feel about young people, let's suppose you're right, that young people haven't been brought up properly. What do we do about it?

Keep in mind that the young people we're talking about are our children, or the children of our children. We must accept some responsibility for what they are. Have we contributed to the problem? We do need more discipline and stronger parental control. The point is, we start where we are and try to get to where we want to be. Our churches and families need to put much greater emphasis on premarital training. People need to understand what they're getting into when they marry. They're not just going to keep house together—there are heavy responsibilities in marriage. We need to take time with them, talk it through, and help them understand the implications of marriage and child–raising.

Young people tend to raise their children as they themselves were raised—and that's frightening. Many people talk a good game but they don't *do* anything. We older adults must give them models to encourage them. When they do things right, we need to tell them they're doing things right. In the teen–

age years, they need discipline and help. I'm trying to be realistic and deal with things as they are. Yes, I feel we need to get back to the Bible and back to its principles. The question is: How do we get there? We surely don't get there by beating and flailing the air, and saying it ought to be this way and why isn't it? That's good exercise, but it doesn't help much. Let's pray for our young people. Let's put biblical principles into practice. God Himself will take it from there!

How Can We Show Understanding?

I realize teen–agers don't want adults to act like kids or imitate their styles, language, fads, and such. But they do want adults to understand them. How can we show the proper understanding, yet clearly remain adults they will respect? How do we talk to them? I've been struggling with this problem for several years and haven't come up with an answer yet. Thanks in advance for your comments.

You are way ahead of many of us with your first statement. Young people *don't* want adults to imitate their life styles. There's nothing quite as pathetic as an aging youth worker who decides to hang on beyond his day. Either he buys a youthful car, or he tries to dress like a kid. Perhaps he tries to talk their language, or maybe he combs his hair like they do. This will alienate and drive young people away more than it will draw them.

There is one quality kids respect above all others, and that is competence. They want to know if you are competent at what you're doing. Are you competent as a grandmother? Would you be a good grandmother? It seems to me adults have bought a completely false theory. We're told that adulthood is out of vogue. When your hair falls out, get some more hair; if it's graying, make it dark again, and so on. There's nothing wrong with growing old—it's part of life. Those wrinkles and gray hairs have been bought at a great price—they are symbols of the experience of having lived life. Age has a certain dignity. The idea that to be eternally young is greatly to be desired is foolish.

None of us want to age any faster than we have to. We all want to enjoy the particular period of life in which we're living—and that's just what kids are interested in. Can you enjoy and be competent at the particular stage of life you're living in right now?

As far as language is concerned, I'd suggest the English language—use it the way you understand it, honestly and authentically. For instance, it's foolish for an adult who wants to talk to young people to use the term, "rap"—they'll wonder what he wants. They don't even use it themselves. Young people understand English, so talk honestly; talk straight from the shoulder; don't talk down to them. Learn to handle pauses and silences. Don't feel you have to talk all the time to make yourself important. When your grandchildren come to grandma's house, give them time to sit and be by themselves and not always be subject to the third degree.

When you do want to know something about understanding young people, ask them how they feel about certain matters. Don't tell them how they *should* feel, but ask them how they *do* feel. Many adults use questions as diplomatic maneuvering rather than saying they want an answer to a question. Young people appreciate straightforward communication from any adult who wants to deal with them.

How Can I Communicate with My Sons?

My wife and I have two sons, seven and five. Now that they are getting older and attending school, I've been thinking about my own childhood and youth. Though my family was quite happy, I do recall times I experienced problems I could not discuss with anyone. My dad tried to help me when I did raise questions, but I was always embarrassed to ask . . . especially questions about sex and relationships to God. In less than ten years, my boys will be at that same stage. What can I do to open the channels of communication now? How can I encourage them to be open as they ask questions or face difficulties?

The emotions you had when you were a teen–ager are probably the kind your boys are going to have. There will be this feeling of reticence, this reluctance to share certain kinds of problems with you as a parent. Naturally you want to help your boys in every area of life. Certain areas of education are better left to the home—certain aspects of living should be held in awe. Intimate sex education is of that type.

Generally speaking, however, a child will feel more comfortable talking to a caring friend, a pastor, a youth pastor, or a favorite teacher than he will with his parents. I'm not talking about the extreme situation where young people are afraid to share *anything* with their parents. They shouldn't be afraid to ask questions of you. This attitude is what you're concerned about.

One more important point: ask more questions than you try to answer. This helps in communication with children. As you ask questions of them, how they feel about things, questions that have this probing quality, then any answer they give is a good one in their eyes. Value the answers the young people give. When you disagree, try to say why you disagree— give your rationale. But don't say to them, "I disagree; now you have to believe like I do." Allow them an opinion. Don't make fun of answers children give to your questions. Don't show contempt by disinterest—children will quickly stop talking to their parents if they feel their parents are looking down on them. Also, don't register shock when they say certain things. Develop a respect for their dignity as persons, at the ages they are now. Begin to listen to their questions now. As you do this, I think you'll find they'll be with you as they grow older.

My Children Have Made Wrong Choices . . .

We have three problems at once! Any help you can give will be most appreciated. Each of our children has made a choice that could affect his future. We do not approve of the choices they have made. We're trying to decide how much we ought to try to influence their decisions. Our daughter, eighteen, has chosen a college; our sixteen–year–old son has chosen a summer job; and our thirteen–year–old is running around with a new gang at school. Should we talk it over with them and let them make the final decision in each case, or should we put our foot down? How can we know when to be firm and when to let go? Thanks for your advice.

The short answer would be yes, I think you ought to discuss the matter with them and let them make the final decision—based on mature alternatives. One of the problems young people have is this: they tend to have difficulty seeing the various sides of an issue. In fact, this could be a good working definition of immaturity: failure to see and weigh alternatives. Young people work on solutions with very few options. The more mature you become, the more options you see. Then you are able to make good decisions. In your case, I would sit down with each one and discuss his or her plans—why he wants to do what he wants to do. Weigh this over against some other alternatives you might think are better. Try to get your children to see the relative merits in the situation.

Remember, some action *you* think is better shouldn't be better for arbitrary reasons. It should be better for some pretty well stated reasons. Your children should see that when they get the matter reduced to its simplest terms—terms they can understand.

There is one line in your letter that intrigues me—the idea of "should we put our foot down?" How do you go about doing this? With a son sixteen years old and a daughter eighteen, I'd wonder how one would do it. For instance, if you did put your foot down, they might refuse to abide by your decision. Instead, think about the actual alternatives. If you can, discuss the matter with friends, when the children aren't around. Perhaps they have faced similar situations. What do we do—tackle them in the front yard, tie them up, chain them to the bed? There really aren't many alternatives except love and logic. As parents you must have built into them at a young age some value structures they can follow when they get to be sixteen or eighteen. So, I'd caution you before you decide to put your foot down to try to figure out where to put it—because you could put it right in your own mouth! That could be difficult!

We all have concerns as parents. But there may sometimes be a desire to manage children's lives. Sometimes I ask myself, why do I want to change my children's lives so much? I realize that I may be unconsciously trying to fulfill my own dream through them. I want them to do something I have not done, or I wish I could have done. Thus I manage their lives in the direction of mine. Other times I fear maybe I haven't instilled in them the proper kinds of values, and therefore I'm afraid to have them go out and try these things. I fear their failure will reflect on me. My failure will be shown up through them. Let me suggest that you take your own suggestion here. Spend some time and discuss the matter with your children—and then help them to make a decision.

My Son Has Different Values . . .

Our eldest son, a senior in high school, came home the other day excited about a movie he had seen in school. It was called "Future Shock." He said that in the future getting married will be out of date. People will live together in communes and share partners. I was shocked by this. When I tried to put over what the Bible says about a husband and wife getting married, he told me that marriage was culturally accepted in Bible times, and in my time, too. In a changing society, however, he says we need to move with the times. Loving others is what really matters. How do I answer that?

By saying that the world is clearly divided into two groups. It always has been, really. There are the people who live in the kingdom of God, and the people who live in the kingdom of this world. People who ignore God, or put God out of their consciousness, are searching for satisfactory ways of living. They question through research, the social sciences, theories —trying to come up with adequate human ways to solve man's problems. As a result of conjecture, speculation, and their own feelings oftentimes (we Christians feel as a result of sin in their lives as well), they come up with certain answers. So films like "Future Shock" make statements like this. The film is predicting—it doesn't say this is the way it ought to be, but this is the way it may be. The Bible says, "Evil men will go from bad to worse, deceivers and deceived" (2 Tim. 3:13 RSV). Indeed, this would appear to be the situation in the world today.

We who are Christians, who are citizens of the kingdom of God, live by another set of rules. We believe that man doesn't discover what is absolute by tests, measurements, social theory, and so on. Rather, an all–loving, all–wise God created us. He has all knowledge about man—He made us, and He knows how to fix us and maintain us. He has given us His revelation, the most loving, sensitive, careful word from Him on how people ought to conduct themselves and live. So He says in His

Book that the best way for people to live together is for a man to marry a woman and take responsibility for her. The man is to treat his wife as Christ treats the church. The wife is to submit herself to her husband because Christ loved the church, and she should see this relationship. Thus they should live together in marriage.

One of the problems those who want to be involved in free love and open marriage have is this: The theory hasn't been tested very long. Give it enough time and we'll see if it really works. At this point, it seems that very few situations like this actually work. The divorce rate is going up—the unhappiness level is at an all–time high. Despite all this, these people are saying this is the better way. Shouldn't things be better then? The Bible teaches that God gives us His revelation from an all–knowing mind. Thus it boils down to deciding which voice you are going to listen to—man's or God's. We side, of course, with God.

Should My Daughter Be a Model?

Our home is in an uproar over a needless decision made by my husband. Our daughter has been offered a chance to be a model—but there is one catch. She is underage. We've looked over the contract and so has our lawyer. It is solid and offers her real opportunity, but my husband refuses to let us falsify her age. She is only one year underage, so I feel he is being too righteous about the whole matter. After all, she's being offered $300.00 a week for just two sessions, and that's a lot of money for a high school girl. Also, it could be the start of something big. She's very beautiful and has a great deal of talent. With her talent, who knows where this could lead?

Who knows indeed? It might lead to something good, but it could lead to something bad. Let's look at both sides. There is the whole problem of your daughter's age. There must be a legal way around this, and your lawyer could probably find it. Obviously children do various kinds of modeling. Look into that aspect.

On the moral side, let's look at your husband's "needless decision." I have a basic distrust of anything built on the wrong foundation. If you begin by manipulating the truth, then when the future comes, you're liable to have some real problems. An old saying applies here: "Sow a thought, reap an action; sow an action, reap a habit; sow a habit, reap a life; sow a life, reap a destiny." If you start at some point in life playing with the truth, in essence you're saying to your daughter, "You ought to be truthful about small things, but when they come in $300.00 packages, you can tell a lie." That puts morality in the marketplace. It puts honesty on the auction block.

Honesty is recognized by all people as a priceless commodity. Remember "Honest Abe"? In his early years before he was President, Abraham Lincoln walked several miles to return a small handful of change to some man he had mistakenly overcharged. We tell that story to our children to point out the value of honesty. Then they come up against a $300.00–per–week decision. Tell them to "fudge" a little bit, and you will undo everything you've tried to instill in them.

I suggest that you make a strong decision here. Say, "No, we'll be upfront and tell the truth. Let's see if the agency can find a way around this." If your daughter has the qualities you describe, the agency will find a way to employ her. You make this decision for the future as well. There are going to be other moral decisions your daughter must make. She may want to bend a little then. If she does you can say, "Honey, we must hold firm on this." If you've held firm at this point, you have established a precedent. If you set a pattern of dishonesty, it will tear down all you've been trying to do.

I recognize how good this opportunity looks—$300.00 is a great deal of money. But don't be misled—there is no price tag on morality.

My Nephew Is a 'Ham' . . .

My nephew has always been a "ham," so it was natural for him to get into theater productions at his high school. His first performance was last Friday night. My husband and I went to see the play with his parents. We were all shocked at the language used in the play. The director could have cut out most of it without affecting the play itself. My brother and his wife are Christians. Now they are afraid their son will pick up some of the filthy language and begin to use it himself. Do you feel they should keep him out of future plays in school?

I don't have enough information to give you a "yes" or "no" answer. This must be a family decision in the light of the facts. But I am concerned about this whole matter. We've all been embarrassed at the language and the innuendoes in school plays. I know these things are considered "adult," and I don't like that either. This whole idea of there being certain things adults do and certain things children do bothers me. Sometimes it is an excuse for adults to act immature and irresponsible.

In many cases, the director *could* cut out the objectionable language without affecting the play itself. This is often true. However, I must in all fairness indicate that portraying reality is sometimes necessary to make a point. Real tension, or real anger may require explicit language. Or the obscene character of a person may need to be portrayed to contrast good with evil. Some language falls into that category. I have friends in the theater who are committed Christians. They have to face this dilemma every day of their lives. There are singers in the Metropolitan Opera who are Christians. They have to face it. Some of our great plays and operas are quite ribald.

We must look at each case individually. Consider the particular piece of literature. Is it worth doing at all? Is it worth filling my head with all these lines in the first place? Does it accomplish any purpose? Is it saying anything? I once saw a play dealing entirely with the subject of adultery. When it ended, no one in the room felt adultery was a good thing. Everyone saw it as an evil thing. It destroyed people, it upset society—it was a ruinous and terrible thing. That was responsible theater. On the other hand, I've seen other plays where adultery was portrayed as "cute." That was irresponsible theater.

These parents must face this situation on an individual level. And their son must face it. If his only motive for acting is that he's a natural ham, that isn't a very good or lofty motive in the first place. If he's interested in acting as a vehicle to express real ideas through theater, then he is a responsible person. You must face all these issues as Christians—and make your decisions carefully and prayerfully.

Why Do Teen–agers Like to Look Sloppy?

We have the challenge of two teen–agers in our home. All things considered, my husband and I think we've done pretty well. I think I understand teen–agers as well as I can, but there are a couple of things I've never been able to figure out. One is, why do they want to look as sloppy as possible? I ask them and they just give me a blank look. Or they give me a profound answer like, "It's in style." Why are recycled jeans in style? My husband and I both work, and between the two of us we bring home a good salary. You can't tell it by looking at our children. I'd be embarrassed to tears except all the other kids look the same. What's the deal? This one has me stumped.

87

I think your child's answer to you is probably correct—sloppiness is in style. That is just as profound as the answer gets. However, if you want to get a little deeper into it, I believe the problem does have some quite meaningful roots. A decade or so ago a strong youth counterculture arose. This culture was a group of people telling us our generation had lost its way. We had our value system centered on the wrong things. We were more interested in things than people, more interested in success than progress; we were more interested in our own welfare than that of others, and so on. So these young people began to attack problems like poverty, war, and racism. And we all agree these things needed attacking—they need solution today as well. One of the ways to attack the problems, the young people decided, was to identify with the downtrodden, the poor, the underprivileged. To work among the poor, they felt they should dress like the poor. If you went to work with farmers in the South, you'd be out of place if you were wearing good clothes when everyone else was wearing work clothes. So, to fit in, the young people began to wear the same clothes.

They were doing precisely what you would do in this situation—you wouldn't go out to a farm to bale hay in your business suit. The philosophy spread to young people not helping in the project. They felt they could help by wearing the same kind of clothing. By doing so they were saying, "I'm part of this, too," though they might not be doing anything to help the poor. Still they were wearing the clothes to say, "I'm identifying with the downtrodden of the world."

This whole attitude caught on. Clothing manufacturers began to see that it was popular for people to wear denim. Now it has taken over—you pay over $20.00 for recycled jeans, successful businessmen wear denim leisure suits, and so on. It means very little today. Young people want to be casual. They want to look like other people.

So much for the history of the matter. I do think there is a positive point that comes out of your letter. You say your kids embarrass you by looking this way. Our children are not dolls we dress up and send out to show our affluence, the "I can dress my kids better than you" syndrome. Looking at a group of young people today, you usually cannot tell who comes from a wealthy home and who comes from a poor home. That's good! We are forced to establish the quality of a person apart from the way he or she dresses. And that's good, too! We have three teen-agers in our home, so I have the same dilemma. Maybe we can weather it together!

I'm Troubled by My Christian Daughter's Friends . . .

A few months ago, one of my dreams came true. My eighteen-year-old daughter received Christ. You can't imagine how happy I was after all those years of praying for her. But now my dream come true is beginning to turn into a nightmare. She's having a terrible time finding good Christian friends. I'd be the first to admit she has tried her best, but so far no success. Now she's talking about going back to her old friends. I'm afraid of this.

I wouldn't be afraid of it. Your concern opens up a scriptural principle not really understood by most Christians. The Christian is intended to be the salt of the earth! Now salt isn't something you would eat by the spoonful. It's only good when it's on something. While salt isn't a basic food, many Christians want to live in the salt shaker! They want to spend all their time with other Christians. This makes them useless to the rest of the world. Salt is only good as it is sprinkled out on the world.

We also understand that an eighteen-year-old needs friends, friends who are compatible. Christian experience has taught us, however, that quite often when a person finds Christ, he finds himself swimming upstream, as it were. When you're floating downstream everything is going in the same direction. You don't run into trouble, and you don't work very hard! But when you turn around, then you bump into things.

Encourage your daughter in this position. Being with friends who have no Christ is exactly where the Lord wants her. This was the prayer the Lord prayed in John 17. Praying for His disciples, He asked, "Lord, I don't pray for these men just to be out of the world, but while they are in it let them account for themselves well." He wanted them to be salt!

Your daughter has the opportunity to be among her friends, but as she is among them, let her express her Christian faith to them. She should be a witness for Christ, the salt of the earth Christ wants her to be.

Sometimes a new Christian finds it difficult to resist the temptation to fall into certain worldly activities. You as her mother and father can provide some prayer support for her. Encourage her, affirm her, support her, help her to sort out some of these moral problems. Help her to walk this new life in Christ among her friends.

Jesus had this particular problem. The Pharisees called Him a wine–bibber, a sinner. They said this of Jesus! Encourage your daughter to think of herself as a physician moving among people who aren't whole. She should ask the Holy Spirit to guide her; she should spend time each day in prayer. Daniel had to pray morning, noon, and night to remind himself he belonged to the Lord, that he had to be loyal to Him. Pray for your daughter while she is with her friends, that her friends may come to see Christ in her.

The Other Students Resent My Daughter's Grades . . .

My daughter has been an A student all through her eleven years of school. She's good, but one thing I don't understand is why some of her friends resent her success. They criticize her for keeping the curve up. Lately the teasing seems to be

*getting her down. It's almost as if they'd like to see her get an
F for once. Then they'd really accept her. It seems ridiculous
to me.*

It is ridiculous, but it is a very real fact of human relations.
In fact, there is a social dynamic that seems to say, "Misery
loves company." Some people can't stand the success of others. One Bible verse is a key to understanding our own spiritual growth: "Rejoice with them that do rejoice, and weep
with them that weep" (Rom. 12:15). A person who rejoices
in other people's sorrow, and sorrows at other people's re-
joicing, is a person in deep trouble. So many people are like
that, aren't they? They really enjoy seeing someone fail rather
than succeed.

This has become so prevalent in our present culture. Even
pastors have learned that to get across certain truths, they
have to lead from weakness. People don't want to hear from
someone who is always succeeding. In some testimony meet-
ings it seems almost a contest to see who can tell about the
worst trouble. People seem to have given up on redemption—
the idea that people can ever be better. We want to submerge
ourselves somewhere down in the golden average, and woe
unto the person who rises above that level.

It is time we realized that excellence is worship unto God.
Excellence in school work, excellence in plumbing, excellence
in every area of our lives is something we need to restore.

To get back to your daughter, perhaps she could be helped
in this way: she excels in scholastic activities, and her friends
can't stand her superiority. So they try to drag her down. Perhaps she can find some strength in them that she can begin
to emphasize. As a result they may feel they can join the
human race and become competitors. It might also be possible
for her occasionally to mention some need of her own. This
will help bring her down to their level. It is hard to relate to
another person who is so obviously superior there is no way
you can help him. A wise person, who is truly superior, finds
ways to allow the weaker person to help him. Perhaps your
daughter and you could think up some ways to reveal her
vulnerability to her friends. Thus she could keep her academic
superiority, but relate to them on other levels.

I'm Worried about My Daughter Driving a Car . . .

My daughter is old enough to drive a car. For a couple of years, I've been trying to get myself ready for this moment in her life. Frankly, I'm disappointed with myself. The thought scares me to death. Just last week there was a tragic accident here in our town which resulted in a fifteen–year–old girl and her seventeen–year–old brother being killed. Their eighteen–year–old friend was seriously injured. I know the law says my daughter is emotionally ready, but my intuition says she's not. Is there any way I can postpone the inevitable?

Yes, I think there is. You can simply say, "You're not driving the car!" However, I understand your feeling. I could have written your letter. My daughter just finished driver education in high school. Now she feels she is ready to drive. As I've tried to look at this objectively, I've come to this conclusion. My daughter has been trained by the school to drive —much more thoroughly trained than I was. When she gets into the car, she's careful to fasten her seat belt, adjust the mirror, seat, and so on. She's ready to drive before she moves that car out of the driveway!

From the human standpoint, I believe that young people are much better prepared to face the total responsibilities of driving than they ever were before. I understand that girls are usually less mechanically inclined than boys, and sometimes we feel they can't handle it as well for that reason. This is not necessarily true.

You ask how you can postpone this moment. But that's not really what you're asking. You just need some help and assurance. She's probably asking to drive all the time. Spend more time preparing her. Let her drive with you in the car. Remember this. After you have done your best, there can still be the fatality on the highway. Sometimes an innocent person is involved in an accident. Some irresponsible person runs into him. A drunken driver perhaps. If we refuse to do anything because of this possibility, we wouldn't get anything done, would we? The safest thing would be to put our children in some kind of vacuum bottle and store them away on the shelf! We know that's silly.

Commit your daughter to the Lord. She's been given to you as a gift from God, sort of on loan to you, anyway. She belongs to the Lord—give her back to Him. Prepare her as best you can through school and your own teachings. Set up some rules, some sensible hours, speed limits, and so on. Then as all parents must do, with much prayer, much fear and trembling, allow her to begin driving. She has been adequately prepared!

Our Son Is Flunking . . .

Could you explain a mystery to me? Last year our son was a beautiful kid—a joy to be around. Now all of a sudden he's flunking at school, fighting with his teacher and the neighbors, and sassing us. We've tried everything. First we ignored him. Then we praised him. At one point we rewarded him. We have tried to reason with him. We have lectured him. We've withheld things. We grounded him. We even spanked him! This has really bothered me because he's fourteen. For six months we've made no progress. Maybe we should ask our minister to talk with him. Any suggestions?

You've about used them all up! I identify with what you're saying. You have tried many approaches with this boy, but you are not making a great deal of progress. Fourteen is an interesting age for a boy. He's not a child anymore. He's no longer cute. He must begin competing in an adult world. Things he used to get away with, people won't allow anymore.

In school he must begin to learn self–discipline. At the age of fourteen, there is more opportunity for self–expression, for handling and managing his own time. This can be pretty frightening to a young lad, and when a person is frightened, he lashes out at those around him. He's lashing out for some reason; he's lashing out at authority. It may be he feels people around him are demanding too much of him. Perhaps he wants more discipline, not less. Maybe he wants more help, not less. It could be he is getting too much freedom too quickly. I don't know the situation, but these are possibilities.

It might be a good idea to have some outside person spend some time with him. This person could be the minister, as you suggest, or a youth pastor. It might be someone closer to his own age. But someone should sit down and just spend time with him, trying to get to the root of his problem.

I'll make a prediction about this boy and others like him. You will try all the things you have already tried. Ministers will talk to him and counselors will work with him. All this will help. But remember this. In growing up, kids go through stages. I wish we could restore that concept to our thinking. Just about the time you've thought up the perfect solution (the psychologically correct solution), he'll suddenly start being a different kind of boy. He'll start talking to people; he'll want a job; he'll become interested in sports and music. Something will happen and he'll suddenly have changed.

Problems such as these are best solved by patience, not panic. If you hold steady, he can be unsteady. I predict he'll outgrow this stage. When you're fourteen sometimes you're just angry at everyone. That's the way it is—but you do outgrow it!

Our Daughter Must Be a Late Bloomer . . .

Our daughter must be a late bloomer. All her friends have suddenly blossomed into womanhood, leaving her and her broomstick figure behind. Just as suddenly, our daughter's personality has changed. She is no longer outgoing, and she avoids her friends. She spends a great deal of time alone in her room. She yells at her little brother constantly. It is getting on everyone's nerves, and there is no solution in sight.

The solution will come. We both know that. It may not come in quite the way and at quite the speed you and your daughter desire, but it will come. Her personality change is probably directly related to the fright and insecurity she is experiencing right now. Let's face it—junior high and high school years are very cruel in many ways. There is a false value system. When young people open a magazine, they see a certain figure considered acceptable. If they don't meet that standard, it is difficult to accept. They feel rejected; they feel they aren't really going to make it. Somehow, they aren't going to fit in.

That is where the family comes in. It must present true values, lifting up people as people, while the world is shouting its false values in the young person's ear. Frankly, I'm quite encouraged that the '70s are so much better than the '50s in this area. At least in literature and the movies today we have the anti-hero. Think of the star, Dustin Hoffman, who is an ordinary looking person, a short man. On TV, heroes and leading ladies are often plain people. This helps a little bit. Back in the '50s, no one could compete with the Clark Gable type. He was completely above us ordinary mortals.

There are some specific ways you can help your daughter during this particular time. First, give her assurances that it will turn out all right. Tell her you love her for what she is right now. I wouldn't say to her, we love you even if you are homely or gawky. You want to get across to her that you love her for what she is. That is much more than her size or shape. Assure her that many other girls have faced her problem. Sometimes children suspect your motives when you are assuring them. They think you say things because you must. You may have a friend among your adult acquaintances, someone both you and your daughter respect. If this person was also a late bloomer, she could share with your daughter how her problems solved themselves with time. This also might be very helpful. There are also magazine articles and books dealing with this problem. Encourage your daughter to read a good book or article, if you find one. See the bibliography for suggestions.

Should My Son Pay Room and Board?

I have a question about raising my children. My son is twenty and working in town, but he still lives at home. We're not poor, but we're not rich either. I'm wondering if it is all right to ask my son to pay room and board. It seems it would help prepare him to be on his own. However, I don't want to give him the impression I'm pushing him. He's the oldest of three boys, so I'm wondering about setting a policy on this.

I had a meeting just the other night where this question came up. I've found an astonishingly small number of parents who liked this "old–fashioned" idea. Less than 10 percent of the couples at the meeting thought board was a good idea. So I told them I disagreed wholeheartedly. I'm a great believer in young people paying room and board after they reach a certain age. We bring on a great many of our problems as parents (especially Christian parents who read the Bible and want to raise children according to its precepts) because we read into the Scriptures things we shouldn't read. We sometimes take adult–to–child advice from the Bible and apply it to people who aren't children at all!

A boy of twenty is no child. He is a man. He could have served in the armed services for two years at that age—or he could be a sophomore in college by this time. He could be a father—so he's definitely not a child! You must approach him on an adult–to–adult basis. He must begin to learn about adult responsibility. After all, the goal of parenthood is to build independence into a child—not dependence. Start when children are small, when they are dependent on us for everything, and then begin slowly to build independence. We must help them stand on their own feet.

If you are fearing this adult relationship, if you prefer the adult–child relationship, I can assure you the adult–adult relationship has a set of rewards all its own. Yes, it is rewarding to have an adult–child relationship, but there are rewards in seeing a child become a man.

Consider your son's economic situation. He would have to go out and pay a certain amount for a room somewhere else. You shouldn't necessarily charge the same amount he'd have to pay in a hotel. He would also have to spend a certain amount for meals, laundry, and other necessities. He could be taking his meals at home for granted. If he had the experience of paying his own way for six months, he would start developing an enlightened gratitude for what's going on at home.

It might be a good idea to show him the costs connected with living. Being a man is not just reaching the age of twenty. It is also accepting a man's responsibility. Room and board can be a great teacher in the school of life. With these three maturing young adults living in your home, you should begin now to teach the lessons of adulthood.

Are Parents Responsible for Their Children's Adult Lives?

A couple of years ago one of your articles appeared in a Christian magazine. The point of the article was that parents can be responsible for how a youngster grows up—good or bad. I did not agree with you then; and now I'm even more sure that I don't. I recently read an article by a psychologist who confirmed my point of view. He said young people who blame their misdeeds on their upbringing are failing to accept responsibility for their own lives. Are you ready to eat crow on this point?

Yes, if we can find this article. One problem with my articles is this: they are almost always edited down. I am quite confident in this particular case that the statement was taken out of context. If it wasn't, then I surely will eat crow on it. However, I don't agree with you completely. Most of us would be willing to accept this fact: our environment has a great effect on what we become. Someone raised in a certain kind of home, in a certain kind of neighborhood, in a certain socioeconomic class, will be affected by this background. Christian parents will affect the behavior of their children. However, they cannot build a fence around their children and predetermine how they are going to turn out.

I've said, and I've been criticized for quoting it, that the Bible declares, "Train up a child in the way he should go; and when he is old, he will not depart from it" (Prov. 22:6). This is not a mathematical formula that builds God into a box. It is a principle of life. In essence, it is saying, "Given all the people who have ever lived on the face of the earth, if they are trained the way they should be (by their parents in Christ), the great bulk of them will turn out the way their parents intended." That doesn't mean there won't be some who go the other way.

There are many spokesmen for the other point of view. Those who believe heredity is the deciding factor tell us that the human being is predetermined by his genes. There is nothing he can do about it. He is completely programmed in advance. Thus, believers in heredity come at us from one direction and the environmentalist comes from the other. I'm one of those people who stand firmly in the middle. You do not destroy human responsibility by pleading environment or heredity. When these two powerful forces come at us from both sides, they don't squeeze us out at the middle! Everyone has a responsibility for his own life. When the umbilical cord is cut, the child becomes an individual—he has his own responsibility and will be judged before God.

The Bible speaks to each individual and demands, "Choose you this day whom you will serve." Jesus talked about a wide gate and a broad way that leads to destruction—and a narrow gate that leads to heaven. Each of us has this responsibility of choice.

To get back to your question—I agree with you. Parents cannot determine their children's destiny. They can't build God into a box and force their children to be perfect by the way they raise them. However, the influence of parents on the life of a child is crucial. Christian example will go much further in influencing a child for Christ than anything else we can do. In that sense we are responsible for our children's destinies.

My Daughter Is Jealous of Her Younger Sister . . .

I have two teen–age daughters. The oldest is eighteen and the youngest, sixteen. The problem is the younger one is really quite pretty and very popular. She could go out every night of the week if I'd let her. The oldest isn't as pretty and outgoing as Susie, and she is extremely jealous of her younger sister. She is really withdrawing into a shell, and I can hardly speak to her at all. I'm growing quite worried about her, but I don't know what to do.

What heartache you are feeling! No two young people are ever exactly alike—even identical twins. One will be more outgoing, the other more withdrawn. There will be other differences, as well. An old commercial used to talk about trading a headache for an upset stomach. In a way your situation is like that. Your problem is twofold. You have one daughter who dates, and one who doesn't. You have one who is well–adjusted, and one who isn't.

Let's take them one at a time: the girl who feels she is plain should be encouraged to understand that variety is the spice of life. Variation in appearance is a fact of our world. Plain girls (whatever that is) get married. Some men are attracted to one girl and some to another. In describing your younger daughter, you put together an interesting couplet, "quite pretty and very popular." It might be helpful for your older daughter to understand that quite pretty and very popular don't necessarily go together. The reason pretty girls are often popular is that they frequently have more self–confidence. They are more outgoing. If your older daughter could be affirmed and encouraged to accept herself as she is, it would help her a great deal. A child like this needs a great deal of affirmation. Spend extra time with her without cutting down your interest in your other daughter. You have to be careful about that aspect as well.

Having made this point, I can only say I don't think any amount of sympathy or advice is going to take away the heartache of reality. You need to sit down with both girls and discuss it. Maybe you have talked it over—but perhaps only in terms of resentment like "I'm tired of her," "I can't stand her," and so on. All three of you should sit down and face the facts. What are the good qualities each has? What are her needs? Give each of your daughters help.

I think the older daughter who is resenting the younger daughter may have another problem. She could be experiencing guilt because of the way she feels toward her sister. Helping her deal with these feelings would also be important. There is a word called "understanding." Reverse it, and it is "standingunder"—giving support. That is what understanding is. Your older daughter needs this desperately, from you and the rest of your family.

My Daughter Blames God . . .

My daughter is in high school now and is going through the stage where appearance is of crucial importance to her and all her friends. I'm afraid she's not very attractive, but we try to buy her nice clothes and suggest flattering make-up hints. What disturbs me is her attitude about her appearance. She has openly told me she blames God for making her ugly and unpopular. She feels He was unfair to her and gave her homely features on purpose. What can I say to her to make her see she mustn't blame God for her appearance?

At the risk of adding to your problem, I must admit your daughter is *right*. God *did* create her. All of us are the result of His mind. One of the important truths to grasp here is that God has made us and not we ourselves. God apparently puts a high premium on individuality, for He made each one of us an individual. We tend to think of these differences as being bad and good. Someone sets up a standard and everyone has to look a certain way. In reality, it would appear that God is only interested in the broad structural differences we have—male and female, tall and short, and so on. We find ourselves caught in the tension between these two criteria when what God has created doesn't fit the norm the world has set up. One's nose is too long, his teeth aren't straight, and so on.

Then we try to conform ourselves to what we're told is the mold of the world. There is even a hint of this in Romans 12:2, "Be not conformed to this world, but be ye transformed. . . ." That's not the primary context from the scriptural viewpoint, I realize. But an overwhelming desire to please the world—to look just like others in clothing and make-up and features—can be an obsession. It reveals that from the inside out, we're trying to please the wrong person.

It is important to realize that each of us is a unique creation of God. When we look in the mirror, we see someone different from all other people. This isn't bad or good; it is just God's mind and plan. We need to discover ourselves. Why does God want a person like me in the world? If I were the only person with these particular features, that would be a problem. Let's say your daughter's problem is that her nose is larger than she thinks it ought to be. All right, she's a Christian girl and has learned from you and from careful observation that she is a unique creation of God, caught up in the world which says that short noses are at a premium. Now she has an opportunity to move out into the world to all the girls with features considered unacceptable by the world's standards and say to them, "Hey, you're being fooled by these standards—you do have value. You are a person. You are a unique creation of God."

It isn't what a certain magazine decides that makes a person good. What makes a person good is whether or not he is following God's path, living according to His will. What you can do to encourage your daughter here is to help her see that beauty is not a matter just of nice clothes and flattering make-up. Beauty is what a person is on the inside. It is an inner beauty of holiness, a commitment to God. Help her to see that it is uniqueness—not difference—we're talking about.

My Son's Best Friend Died . . .

Last month one of my son's best friends drowned. Jerry is fifteen and is taking it very hard. He has lost weight. He has no interest in athletics, or anything else. Maybe this is normal and temporary, but I can't help feeling it is partly my fault. I did nothing to prepare him for this kind of thing. Is there some way we can prepare our children for experiences like this?

We like to think we send people to college to prepare them for life, jobs, etc., but the truth is if we haven't faced life in its entirety, including death and eternity, we haven't faced reality. We have done a great deal to insulate people from death. A generation ago, a son often helped to dig his father's grave, or he dressed his parent for burial. That was quite an experience. Doubtless it brought people close to death and the experience of death. In a rural society young people are constantly in contact with animals. They see them die and experience the heartache and reality of it all. An urban young person has no brush with death at all. The death of an insect may be all he's ever experienced.

Instead of people dying, they "pass away" today. We don't go to graveyards—they are cemeteries. All this may insulate us from reality.

The Bible tells us that man's life is like a vapor. Death is a reality. God wouldn't have put realities in His Word if He didn't want us to deal with them. I think we do need to prepare young people for death. We need to take them to funerals. Children six or seven years old may be too young. However, if it is someone close to them, even six or seven may not be too young. When a person gets into high school, he should not avoid realities.

To get back to your son. It's possible he is morose because he has an unresolved conflict with the drowned boy. The Bible tells us, "Don't let the sun go down upon your wrath." It might be well to sit down with your son and discuss this with him. Is there tension between him and other people, his parents perhaps? Get these matters out into the open. He should be forgiven so he won't have to deal with regrets later on.

One of the deepest emotions a young person can feel is to lose his parent or a friend to death. And this is compounded if he thinks, *Oh, I wish I had said something*. Perhaps your son can use this as a learning experience, to prepare him for the future.

Extended Family Relationships:
Part Three.
In-laws and Out-laws

My Sister Borrows Things and Doesn't Return Them . . .

I've been fortunate. I grew up in a close family that loves the Lord. All of us have married and are still living in the same town. It is a miracle in this day of great mobility. Living close to family members does have it disadvantages, though. For instance, my sister is forever borrowing things—like special cooking utensils, or records, or even some big things like our portable stereo. The problem is, she never returns them after she borrows them. She stops by and it's always, "Oh, I forgot to bring it back." I almost have to take my belongings back forcibly. We could stop loaning her things, but she'd just go to someone else and the same thing would happen. Couldn't we help her break this habit and become more considerate?

Apparently this problem runs in families—it might even be a contagious disease! Many people are afflicted with it. Most of us are reluctant to deal with things as they are. We should just sit down with that sister or brother and simply say, "Hey, I have a problem. My problem is irritation. I'm getting irritated because I've spent money on these things, which I'm very happy to lend you. But I need them when I need them. That's why I bought them. You are irritating me by not returning them, not by borrowing them." That's what needs to be said.

You might be surprised at what could happen. Your sister might not have thought of this. Probably she does not realize it is this important to you. She doesn't appreciate that you need these things. You don't use them every day, but when you want them, you expect them to be there. Deal with this problem in a forthright manner. You might tell her when she borrows something, that you need it right back. Ask her to bring it back by a certain time. Settle the whole agreement on the spot—that could help. Take the ambiguity out of it.

I've asked myself, why do people deal with this problem so indirectly? Why don't we confront people with these things? One reason is that we don't seem to be able to discuss issues without discussing personalities. We need to learn to be upset at a specific situation without being upset at the person involved. If we don't, we create a worse problem—feelings of resentment, gossip, and so on. If we dealt with the problem straight–on, this wouldn't happen.

Your sister needs to know that in rejecting the idea of borrowing things, and not returning them, you are not rejecting her. You still love her—she's your sister, and you're not going to drive her out of your family. But you do expect that she will show more respect for your possessions. My advice is to be very open and honest with her. You might be delighted at her positive response.

How Do We Settle My Mother's Estate?

My mother died last month after a short illness. It was quite sudden and a shock to all of us. Dad died several years ago. After the funeral was over, my brother, sister, and I went about settling the estate. Mother specified that we three were to divide up the household possessions we wanted among ourselves and sell the rest. That's the problem. There are many memories tied to those things, and it has been especially difficult to settle on who gets what. I never thought I'd be arguing with my own family about mom's possessions. Can you suggest any way we can settle this fairly without acting so greedy and getting into long–lasting arguments?

This problem occurs in some very fine Christian families. People's emotions are close to the surface at times like this.

Dividing up personal possessions without having hurt feelings is a real art! What are possessions really? In a way, possessions and money are extensions of ourselves. That's why they are so dear to us. When the Bible tells us: "Where a man's treasure is, there will his heart be also," it is speaking the truth. Not only is it a good guideline for living the spiritual life, it is also a good thermometer to test where we are spiritually.

Abraham and Lot are a good illustration of this. Abraham was the man of God, and Lot was selfish. Abraham chose the lesser possession after Lot chose the better. Jesus, too, spoke about our acquisitive natures. He said, "If a man asks you for your coat, give him your cloak also." The Bible says that the Christian should not be greedy and acquisitive. The Christian should not be selfish. God will take care of him.

In your situation, give in for the greater good in some of these areas. After all, your mother was not a dish, or a bowl, or a knick-knack. Your memories of your mother are the real and lasting things. The love you shared is the important thing. Is having some dish in your china cupboard at the expense of your relationship with your brother and sister worth it? Give in to maintain harmony. Trust God in this situation. If your mother were to observe this whole episode—and there is some scriptural indication that she might—she'd be proud of you for having given up some material things for the greater good. It is more important to keep the family together and help your weaker brother and sister to grow in grace. Be an example to them and show Christian grace in their presence.

My Wife Is Becoming an Interfering Mother-in-law . . .

I hate to say it, but I think my wife is becoming an interfering mother-in-law. My son was married four years ago. Now he and his wife have a two-year-old son. They are, of course, much more modern and up-to-date than my wife and I are, so my wife doesn't like the way they are raising Mark, the boy. She makes sly little comments and I can see my daughter– in–law resents them. I asked my wife not to say anything, but she says she can't help it. I want to stop this before it gets out of hand.

If you spent time at a conference for grandparents, the bulk of the conversation would probably deal with this very problem. It is difficult for grandparents to identify with the way young people want to raise their children. This isn't necessarily because the young people are right or wrong. In many cases, the grandparents are just wishing they had done some things differently themselves. Now they are much more experienced and they think, *Boy, if I could get another crack at it, I'd do better this time.* And they probably would. The only problem is most people become parents in their early married years, before they get a chance to gain all this experience.

Perhaps your wife feels she has learned some things that would be helpful to your son and his wife. It isn't so important whether she is right or wrong. The question is, should she interfere? Why don't you and your wife sit down and talk about this? Encourage her where she is right in this situation —but ask her if it is always good to share being right with the children. Maybe she could help them more by praying for them—by affirming the things they're doing correctly rather than by always finding fault. This way she will feel she has an ally in you. Yet you can advise her about interfering and keep her out of the situation.

Many modern parents are afraid of their children—afraid to discipline them. The best way you can help is to provide a climate of encouragement, love, and affirmation. Admire the good things your son and daughter–in–law do, and share (very carefully) advice in private. You don't want to create the impression that "just because dad says it, it must be old-fashioned." Some principles never go out of style or out of date. God's way of raising families is one of these things!

Should My Mother Live with Us?

Our family is facing a dilemma. My mother has been crippled by arthritis and is not able to work any more. She cannot even get around very well by herself. We are thinking of inviting her to live with us. We feel strongly about helping our parents when they need it. After all, they stuck by us through thick and thin. However, my mother, who is a widow, has been grouchier and less tolerant toward our children the last few years. We are torn between neglecting my mother, or making it tougher on our children.

This problem enters most of our lives in one form or another. Really it is a cultural question—what do we do about the aging? Personally I feel that for the church and concerned Christians, this may well be one of the biggest challenges ahead of us. There is so much emphasis put on young people, church growth, Christian education, and so on. Now we are faced with growing numbers of senior citizens. What do we do as responsible families and churches? People do grow older and simply cannot care for themselves. It is surely unchristian to think in terms of discarding them. Some of the greatest resources we have in all the world are locked up in the lives of older people. They have experience and tremendous insight that need to be tapped. I'd suggest that even the tone of your question reveals difficulty.

Though I don't want to be critical of you, you are underestimating your mother—she is able to deal with her problem herself. You should sit down with her and tell her *your* problem. Your children are small and because they are small, they are active. They do the things small people do. Not only are they small people, but they are *human* small people, and they probably have faults. Point out that as parents we all have faults. Therefore, your home has certain problems in it. You are trying to do the best you can, but doing the best we can is not always ideal. Tell her, "We love you. We have room in our home for you, and we'd like to have you come. We know that with your arthritis there is pain and also frustration. Our fear is this—that your coming into the home is going to cause a tremendous strain for us because you are going to be demanding that the child act in an abnormal way. So if you come, there has to be give and take."

If you put it this way, and take the time to discuss it thoroughly, you might be surprised at how well your mother understands your situation. She might be able to respond to it very constructively. Perhaps no one has told her how grouchy she's become—maybe she doesn't want to be that way. This is an individual situation. The answer may be to put your mother in a home where she can be cared for full time, where people are knowledgeable about her physical condition. On the other hand, it is possible that your children could gain a great deal by having their grandmother in your home, by seeing how one deals with frustration and pain. It could be one of life's great lessons for them. They shouldn't reject discomfort because it has pain in it. Living sometimes involves pain. This is a lesson they need to learn.

My Children Are Embarrassed by Their Grandfather . . .

My parents have lived on the west coast all their lives. Just recently my mother passed away and we decided to bring my dad to live with us for a while, until we could place him in a good home in the area. We were prepared for some problems, but not this kind. Grandpa is an invalid, and he is pretty cranky much of the time. I get exasperated with him once in a while myself. But the children have really bothered me. They complain about having him around and more or less ignore him when he talks to them. I think it is just rude to treat him like that, but the kids say they are embarrassed to have their friends over. They feel he is disrupting the whole

*family. It is partly true, but I still think people in this day
and age should learn to respect old people. I thought my
children were different, but I guess they aren't. What can I
do to help them?*

In the Old Testament the prophets and leaders had to speak
to people on the subject of honoring father and mother. Even
in those ancient days people wanted to put the old folks out
of their homes, thus breaking down the patriarchal structure.
In effect they were saying, "It's a pain in the neck to have dad
around because he still wants to run the ranch—and I've in-
herited it. I'm running it, so why should he call the shots?"
So God issued a commandment that says, "Honor thy father
and mother," speaking about the care of old people and showing respect in the home.

In your letter you mention that you feel young people
should learn to respect old age. It's more than that. The
emphasis should not be just on respect for old age, but respect
for people. Your children need to find a way to respect
grandpa, not a way to respect old age. That in itself is patron-
izing. One of the things that irritates old people the most is to
be treated like children.

Often we adults tend to do this same thing with old people
—pat them on the back and lead them around. Here's a man
who was once a leader, a family man, a breadwinner. Now he
is being treated like a child. In his autobiography, one great
Christian writer mentioned that more and more he found
people talking down to him, as if he were a three-year-old.
This was demeaning.

You should respect your father yourself. Then tell your
children who he is. Tell them about him when he was at his
best. He deserves your respect and theirs. Help them to see
him as a person, not just an impotent pile of flesh. This is the
best way you can help them—and him!

Interpersonal Relationships:
Part Four.
Who Is My Neighbor?

We're Concerned about Our Friends' Children . . .

My husband and I are really concerned about this other couple. They are our best friends—we even double-dated in high school. We were as close as could be. It is kind of a laugh really how we ended up in the same community after we were married. But it has been great because we have so many things in common. We're very outdoorsy. The men know practically every fishing stream in the state. Alice and I do everything together. That is, we used to do everything together—before we had children. That's when the problems started. My husband and I believe in being really strict with our children, but Jack and Alice are pretty easygoing. In fact, they let their kids run wild. It wasn't so bad when they were babies, but now we each have two pre-schoolers, and what a difference! We can't even carry on a conversation when their kids are up. It's like a circus. We really like Jack and Alice, but we find ourselves going over there less and less because they just can't control their kids. What are we supposed to do? Can we say, "Let us tell you how to handle your kids"? So far we haven't had the nerve. What should we do?

I receive quite a few letters like this. It seems to be one of the major areas of contention between good friends . . . differences in attitudes toward childrearing.

It may be that your friends haven't noticed these things about their children. People have different tolerances for noise, confusion, upset, and so on. One person may have an obsession for organization, keeping things picked up. Another may not be concerned about neatness at all. So perhaps these two people really haven't noticed the problem with their children as you have. Talking about it openly may be a real help to all of you.

It may be that after you have discussed the matter you will simply disagree. They may feel you are too concerned—you may continue to feel they are too loose. Maybe your friendship will have to be outside of the children. I know of situations like this where couples simply get together as couples because bringing their children together creates a problem. Maybe twenty years from now both couples will look back and see where they have erred in one way or another.

You have to set your pattern for childraising and follow it. Decide what you believe and stick with it, realizing that ultimately you're going to live with the result. Don't let your good relationship with this couple be disrupted by this situation. The first thing to do is what you say you're afraid to do—but if you discuss this openly you might be surprised at how much agreement you really have.

I Offended a Fellow-Christian

I'm the Sunday school superintendent in my church. A month ago at a teachers' training session, I used one of my primary teachers as an example of how not to discipline a child. She had shared an incident earlier with me. On the spur of the moment, I related it to the group. Later I discovered I had embarrassed her. She was furious with me. I apologized to her privately, and publicly at the next meeting, but she still shows no sign of being willing to forgive me. What more can I do?

There is little you can do really, except maintain a willingness to accept your responsibility for the harm done in this case. When you have offended someone like this, and you've sought forgiveness, both publicly and privately, then the responsibility shifts to the other person. Forgiveness is a two—way street. It involves not only a forgiver, but also one who is being forgiven. Christ forgives us our trespasses, as the Lord's Prayer tells us, and we are supposed to forgive those who trespass against us. So in this case, the lady simply needs to understand that forgiveness works both ways.

The Bible speaks to this whole issue. It tells us the tongue is an unruly evil, full of deadly poison. Who can tame it? That is a rhetorical question. The implication is that very few can. It is something we have to learn, sometimes at a cost of great embarrassment and pain. You're experiencing these stresses now. My guess is that this will make a lasting and lifelong impression on you. All of us learn our lessons in this way. I've suffered a good many times from hoof-in-mouth disease—saying something before I got my brain in gear.

In addition to the Bible, I've found another set of slogans helpful. These were written by a Christian man for the Rotary Club. I call this my "4-way test." You ask yourself the question, is this true? Then, is it fair? Then, is it beneficial to all concerned? And, will it build lasting friendship? I've found these questions helpful. The Holy Spirit can bring those to my mind while I'm waiting to make my next statement sometimes. He may touch my heart and say, "Hey, that could be left unsaid." "You don't need to say that." Or, "Have you checked that out with the person concerned?"

There is a certain danger connected with being open . . . sharing in the church, testimonies, and so on. Do I have the permission of the other person before I share his problems? Confessing our own sins, that's one thing. But sharing those of others isn't openness—that is irresponsibility. It is invasion of privacy. Your experience is a good lesson for all of us. Understand and apply the Scriptures to your interpersonal relationships.

My Neighbor Finds Fault with My Children . . .

My next-door neighbor is a good Christian and my good friend. We have a lot of fun together, except when it comes to our children. The problem is that she never notices anything her kids do wrong, but she is always pointing out the mistakes and faults of my children. When you have a problem like this, what do you do? I've tried ignoring it. And I've tried praying about it. It is beginning to bother me so much that I hate to see her coming over in the morning.

We don't solve our problems by ignoring them. You need to share your feelings openly with your neighbor. I'd recommend an excellent book, *Caring Enough to Confront,* by David Augsburger. He recommends confrontation as a worthwhile practice in the Christian life. Sometimes we can't discuss truth in any other way. Augsburger indicates that being a doormat isn't necessarily spiritual. There are many people who have the idea that a Christian is someone who is kind of namby–pamby. He crawls between the mattress and the springs and says, "I'm a worm, step on me." Augsburger points out that a Christian ought to share his views with the other person.

It appears in this particular situation that you have two different standards for your children. These are: "A good child is a curious and creative child." One mother says, "This child is misbehaving because he doesn't seem to be disciplined." The other mother says, "This is a bad child because he really doesn't seem to be interested in things. He isn't curious and creative." What is precocious to one is beautiful to the other. You are probably looking at the children from different perspectives. Perhaps you ought to point this out. You might say, "I appreciate your pointing out these things, but here's how I've felt about your children. Why do we feel differently?"

You'll probably find that your children are somewhere between good and bad—that is, yours are not perfect, and neither are hers. Yours are not bad, and neither are hers. You are simply measuring them by different standards. Her children apparently are measuring up to her standards, but not to yours. So this is confusing.

Family Finances:

Part Five.

Where Does All the Money Go?

We Wonder Where Our Daughter Is Spending Her Money . . .

Our high school daughter has been receiving an allowance of $1.00 per week for the past few years. Just this year, however, she has been babysitting in the neighborhood and often earns as much as $10.00 a week. Since we provide all her clothing and school expenses, her father and I are beginning to wonder where all this money is being spent. She says she gives 10 percent to the church and the rest is her own. In effect she is saying it is none of our business how she spends it. What does a parent do in this situation? We're sure there are temptations to buy cigarettes, or beer, or even drugs at school, so how can we deal with this? How much right do we have to regulate her use of the money she is earning on her own?

The other night I had a meeting with a group of parents. I asked them how many gave their children an allowance. About 40 percent gave an allowance. The rest doled out money informally to their children. That was kind of a revelation to me. I assumed that almost every parent was involved in allowances. That night I made quite an appeal for the value of the allowance system as a learning experience for children. It teaches them responsibility.

You have been getting by with a very easy arrangement—$1.00 per week for several years. By today's standards, that isn't much money for a young high school student to have. Such a limited amount might even force her to do some unacceptable things—such as selling her possessions, borrowing, gambling, and so on—to get more money. This could lead to worse problems. On the positive side, you should be quite happy your daughter is babysitting and earning money on her own. That is commendable. She is giving 10 percent to the church. That puts her in the top 2 or 3 percent of the entire American public. Only about 2 or 3 percent of church people tithe. She deserves your praise on that score.

Your question is, should you regulate the money she has earned on her own? I don't feel that you should. That money is her own. She should learn the penalty for squandering it, spending it unwisely, and so on. This leads me to your other comment about her clothing and school expenses. Why not allow her to pick up some of her school expenses first? Say, "All right, if you have more money to spend, now we'll ask you to buy more of the things you want at school." Begin to de-escalate your financial involvement as her contribution grows. In this way you will find you can teach your daughter financial responsibility. Taking over the management of the money she earns would have the opposite effect. It would break down the relationship of trust you are trying to build. As she increases her ability to earn, you may decrease your involvement in her financial affairs.

My Husband Uses a Credit Card for Everything . . .

My husband and I just had another argument about money. Actually, it wasn't really an argument. Bill is always very understanding about the way I feel. The annoying thing is he never changes. Bill uses a credit card for everything. He doesn't like to carry cash. He claims you can keep a more accurate record of your spending if you use credit. My father was just the opposite. He paid cash for everything. He thought credit cards were dangerous—the main cause for people living above their means. Well, that is exactly what has happened to us. Bill just took out another debt consolidation loan. That's the reason for the argument. Now he says we're all fixed. He seems confident, but I'm afraid we're not going to be able to make ends meet. Isn't there a verse in the Bible about not going into debt? I just don't think it is right for Christians to get involved with obligations like this, but what can I say to make my husband understand?

This letter reminds me of a cartoon. The man from the loan office was saying, "Consolidate your bothersome little bills into one great staggering overwhelming debt!" This is what many people find themselves doing today.

Let's clear up one misconception. Is the use of credit cards sinful? I think credit cards, like other objects, are incapable of sin. There is a tendency among people always to try to deny human responsibility and blame it on something else: alcohol, credit cards, TV, etc. These inanimate things are incapable of sin. Sin is a moral issue—irresponsibility is a moral issue. Credit cards can be used by people to live beyond their means. Easy credit does, in that sense, encourage people to overspend. But I guess a checkbook can do the same thing, can't it? That's why some people don't keep their stubs up to date—they are afraid of the math.

Perhaps credit cards aren't the problem here. Your father's diagnosis could be correct. The credit cards don't cause people to live recklessly. Their lack of discipline causes that. Your family has a problem. Your husband is doing the spending, and you are doing the worrying. It might be wise to put the worrying in his lap as well. I get many letters dealing with this particular subject. It seems to be the cause of many problems in marriage. The same person doing the spending should be doing the worrying! Make him write the checks and pay the creditors. That will have a good effect on him, I think.

Sit down with Bill and discuss why you are not demanding this. Tell him you would be happy with less. Make this a family slogan: "What ever happened to make–do?" Let's try to make–do with what we have. What could we keep from buying this month? This new direction in your thought pattern would be more effective than tearing up the credit cards.

What Can You Do with a Wife Who Spends Too Much?

What can you do with a wife who spends too much? I've tried all kinds of ways to control it, but I don't want to be a dictator.

Whenever I give her a little freedom, she goes out and buys everything she can. If it wasn't for this, we'd have a very happy marriage.

Maturity is the ability to postpone gratification. Keep in mind there is a multi–million–dollar advertising industry out there trying to convince us that this definition is wrong. They are saying, "Get what you want right now—buy now, and you won't have to pay for it until next February—we'll spread out the payments so you won't feel it." Most of us have found out that you *do* feel it all too soon.

Don't be too hard on your wife in this situation. She simply may have become a pawn in this clever scheme to get everyone to live beyond his means. Apparently your wife doesn't understand how much money it takes to run the family. The two of you should sit down together and discuss this situation. Analyze how much money you have available—divide it into categories. Show her how much it takes and how it all adds up together. I would give her a certain amount for groceries and other expenses. Beyond that, you'll have to be fairly firm. Allow cause and effect to take its course. If she chooses to blow her household money on frivolous things, you won't have enough to make it through the week. It might be helpful to get through a week with just basic staples. She will find out that when the money runs out, it runs out.

There are people who are just emotionally unable to handle money. Or maybe your wife has followed a wrong bit of logic —that ownership of things brings happiness. With more things you can be happy. You might spend time discussing why she needs these things. Emphasize the things that don't cost money but do bring happiness. Maybe she feels she isn't really accepted by you. Perhaps she feels she's only accepted if she has a new dress. You compliment her only when she gets her hair fixed. You only notice those extras that cost money. Start noticing the basic things and see if that doesn't help. Perhaps you can reverse this trend toward purchasing things to bring happiness. You already have a happy marriage. Honest discussion of these issues could make it even happier!

Part Six. **Dating and Sex:**

Where Do We Go from Here?

We Worry about Our Son Being Alone with His Girl Friend . . .

Our son and his girl friend have been dating about six months. They've been welcome at our home. During the summer they came here a lot. Lately they've been going elsewhere. When we ask our son, he says, "We'll be at Linda's house." And that's the problem. Her parents both work. It seems dangerous for these two kids to be alone there. What shall I do?

I agree—it is dangerous for them to be alone at Linda's. However, if you mention it to your son, he'll reply, "Dad, you're just being suspicious." If your son does counter with this accusation, it will give you an excellent opportunity to discuss the whole matter. Your reply could be, "Son, you're right. I am suspicious. Let me tell you why. I'm a man just as you are. Let me tell you about myself." You could then go on to confess to your son that you understand sexual tendencies and temptation. That might be a tremendous revelation to him! When you tell a boy you've had sexual temptations . . . he doesn't think of his father as a sexual person. He assumes that somehow he dropped in from a cloud somewhere. Other kids were born down at the hospital, but he wasn't. He never thinks of you and your wife as sexual partners. Children don't view their parents that way.

The experience of mankind up until now has been that when people put themselves in the wrong situations, they sometimes open the door to experiences they cannot handle. Make it clear to your son that you aren't really suspicious of *him*, but of mankind in general. Male and female are put together differently. This was God's idea. To recognize it is not to have a dirty mind or to somehow be suspicious of your son. You're just facing up to reality.

Then I'd go on, "Why don't you talk to Linda's dad about it? Ask him if he thinks it's a good idea for you to be around there alone for three or four hours at a time." Linda's father may give your son some help here. He may have some comments to make. As soon as you suggest that he talk to Linda's dad, your son will get the point! He will understand what you are trying to say.

Continue to make your son and Linda welcome in your home. Make it possible for them to have privacy—but keep an eye on them. They don't need to be spied on, of course.

I'd surely make this clear to him, "If Linda's parents don't care, we do. Why? Because we respect you and want to help you respect yourself. We respect the reality of your sexuality." If you take this approach, I think you will be successful.

I Don't Know What My Son Does on His Dates . . .

My problem is simple. I don't know what my son does on his dates. I usually know who he's with, and where they plan to go, but I have no idea what goes on. Should I? I have talked to some of the men in the church about it, and most of them are just as much in the dark as I am. They seem to hope their sons are behaving—and most of them probably are. I trust my son, but I don't want to be naive either. My father never asked me questions about this sort of thing, and frankly I don't think it ever entered his mind that I might need some guidance. That was another era. What about today?

Reading between the lines, I think you are ambivalent about this. You trust your son, but in a way you don't. I don't think you need to know what goes on during his dates. You do need to trust your son. Somewhere in his life there is a line. He's drawn it as a result of his value system, and he's said, "I won't go beyond that line." This line exists in every person's life. Some have it so far back you can hardly find it. Others have it right up in front. Your son has been raised in a responsible home.

The best advice I've ever seen on this whole subject comes from Paul who wrote, "Continue thou in the things which thou hast learned" (2 Tim. 3:14). He also said, treat "the younger (women) as sisters, with all purity" (1 Tim. 5:2). If I say that to a group of high school kids, I'm sure to get a laugh. But they know what Paul is saying. He views his sister as a person—he doesn't see her as an object or a thing. He respects her—he knows she loves and fears and anticipates, that she is fragile and has feelings. We understand these things about our sisters, but men sometimes think about other girls as if they were just things, sex objects, ways to get gratification for themselves.

If a boy is taught to respect other people, including girls, as creations of God, as persons rather than objects, he will treat the girl he is with as a person rather than an object. I think of the crude phrases young people use to describe their relationships. Almost always they imply *getting* for oneself—rather than sharing and responsibility.

For the record, I've worked with young people for twenty years, and it seems to me that today's high schoolers are much less involved in sexual intimacy than they were even in the '50s. Today's kids play it cooler than the generation just past.

My Son's Girl Friend Is Too Aggressive . . .

My seventeen–year–old son is dating a girl who is quite aggressive. She is constantly calling him on the phone. Recently she even suggested that they go steady, and my son went along with it, not knowing what else to do. He does not want to hurt her feelings. As a mother, what kind of advice can I give him? Though he talks to me easily about their relationship, I'm stumped as to what I can say.

I wonder if your son really understands this relationship. He's pretty ambivalent about the whole thing. First of all, having a girl friend is sort of fashionable in high school. Going steady puts you in a certain category. Having a girl friend also ties one down, and often boys find they aren't ready to be tied down. The girl friend becomes a ball and chain in that case.

In this situation, I suspect you also have the problem of uneven maturity. On the one hand, your son may be a symbol of some sort of success to her. She may need to feel the security of a steady boy friend. Your son happens to be it.

On the other hand, she may be more mature than he is. She is ready for this sort of relationship, but he isn't. He may feel he's just being dragged along, used. An alcoholic once told me that he never received any help until he became sick and tired of being sick and tired! If your son feels cornered by the girl, he needs to face it and say to her, "I like you; I enjoy being with you; I like the idea that you like me. But I really don't want to be trapped. Can't we just be friends? Can't we just see each other without going steady?"

If the girl is unable to accept that, then the relationship will break off. Or she may accept it but still want to possess him —own him. So he still won't be free. Help him to have the courage to deal with this problem. Assure him that the right girl will come along when he's ready for a deeper commitment. A close attachment now will simply lead to frustration. He's not ready for it educationally, economically, or emotionally.

Your son needs to understand that his relationship is his own doing. The only way he can correct it is by positive action on his part.

My Daughter's Boy Friend Is Too Old for Her . . .

My daughter is fourteen. While she may look a little older than that, she thinks she is a lot older. The problem is she has a boy friend who is eighteen. She says she loves him and wants to go out with him all the time. He's really not the type of boy friend we would have chosen for her. She is also much too young to be getting so serious. How can we get her to forget about him? I'm afraid she may be sneaking out with him, so I really want to put a stop to this.

There's quite a difference between fourteen and eighteen! At twenty and twenty-four it wouldn't be so bad. At fourteen your daughter is definitely immature in relation to an eighteen–year–old boy. An eighteen–year–old is a young man. At fourteen your daughter is just entering adolescence. On the other hand, puppy love is very real to the puppy! At this particular stage of life, being against the romance isn't going to stop it.

First of all, let me suggest that you sit down and talk to the young man. At eighteen he should understand some things that a fourteen–year–old girl doesn't understand. For one thing, if he is going to go with your daughter, you are going to have to restrict their relationship because of her age. Personally, I wouldn't allow a girl of fourteen to go out alone in a car with a boy. Tell him that if he is going to date her, he will have to date her at home around the family. That should cool him off a bit. Then I'd suggest you limit the number of visits per week. While she's in school, she has to study, she needs rest, and so on. He can probably live with more late nights because he's older.

Perhaps you could talk to the two of them as to what is ahead for them. She's fourteen. She feels she's "head over heels" in love. And she's going to marry him. How soon? Most girls wouldn't want to get married before the age of eighteen. So they have perhaps four years. Does he really want to wait that long? Does he really love her? If he does, then the kind of restrictions we've talked about must be enforced. If he's willing to live with those, I'd respect him for that. On the other hand, if the period of waiting looks too long to him, then I'd suggest that maybe he find someone nearer his own age.

How can you make your daughter forget him? You can't. She'll cry and try to punish you. She'll stare out her bedroom window and pout. But she'll live through it. As a Christian parent, you must assume your responsibility in this situation. Tell her, "Honey, we're doing this because we love you." But be firm as well as loving.

When Should My Daughter Begin Dating?

What do you think is the best time for a girl to start dating in this day and age? My daughter is fifteen. When I tell her I think she is too young, she screams her head off that I'm old–fashioned. Maybe I am, but it seems to me that fifteen is too young. If I'm wrong I wish you would tell me and also tell me when a girl should start dating. I have three younger daughters at home!

I note your phrase, "this day and age." This idea has become a fetish—it's as though this day and age has changed everything. Are things so different now than they used to be? No. Things, many of them, are the same. In fact, I'd venture to say that girls and boys growing up today are somewhat the same as they were when you were a girl. Yes, there are differences —different temptations, different information, more sophistication perhaps. Children understand some things we wish they didn't understand, but this day and age doesn't change the situation that much.

Let's look at your fifteen–year–old daughter. What's her maturity level? Bible scholars tell us Mary wasn't more than fifteen when Jesus was born. In that day, women of that age were married. The idea of dating itself is a Western idea. I've traveled around the world and people fear the Western idea of dating. In two–thirds of the world marriages are arranged and the divorce rate is lower in those countries than in ours.

Let's look at some other factors. In our day people sort of shop around to find the person they are going to marry. It's foolish to try to live back in the Bible days—we live now. How can your daughter handle a dating situation? How mature is she emotionally? How does she handle herself in difficulties? If you tell her she can't date, she "screams her head off." This is a pretty good indication of her maturity level. And she needs to be told that. Someone who can't handle a simple "no" about a date surely couldn't handle any of the deep problems that come up in dating life.

At our house, we decided at fifteen years old a girl ought to be able to date a boy one grade older than she is. We've bent that on occasion—for a boy we've known as a family. But we feel young people ought to date in groups at that age—go with other couples. Sixteen is early enough to date with one boy and one girl in the car. I'd still prefer that they would go in a group! I want to know where they are going, what time it gets out, and how much time there is between when it gets out and they get home!

These are the things I'm concerned about as a father. Analyze these matters according to your daughter's situation. All parents face this problem, and we face it together. There are no cut-and-dried rules—but we do have custom and common sense on our side!

I'm Worried about the Church My Son Is Attending . . .

My son has a new girl friend. I think he's quite serious about her. Sonya is a nice girl, but she goes to a different church, certainly not one we would have chosen for him. The problem is that my son has decided he is going to that church. I'm sure it'll last only as long as he goes with Sonya, but it still bothers us. It would bother us more if they decide to marry and become members of that church. I'd like some way of stopping this but I don't know how.

Psychology being what it is, and people being as they are, one way you can be sure to encourage this romance is to stand against it. Don't make a scene and tell him he can't go! Young people in their teens often like to experience other types of worship experiences. Not long ago a study was conducted among Christian college students. Young people were asked what church they attended when they went away to college. The answers showed that young people who came from rather informal churches tend to choose more formal churches when they go away. The reverse was also true. Perhaps your son is just enjoying a different type of service. My guess would be, however, that he's enjoying Sonya! He likes to be with her. Where she is, is where he's going to be for a while!

Now on this matter of church and where we go to worship. Let's establish this fact: there is a wideness in God's mercy. The important thing is not modes of worship but the gospel! Is this a church where the gospel is being preached and the Bible is revered? Authority is important. Biblical Christians do worship God in various ways. Your boy is going to have to find a church according to his individual choice. The Bible says, "Choose you this day whom you will serve." Parents can't choose for their children. Young people have to choose for themselves.

If the church which Sonya attends is an empty place where the gospel is not preached, nothing is happening there. Your young people will discover that emptiness quite soon. They will not continue to return to a table where they are not being fed. If *your* church is the kind of place where the gospel is being preached and there is spiritual food, then they will come where they are fed. The gospel is a powerful force in this world. Once a person knows Christ as his Savior he'll develop a thirst for the gospel and come back to where it is being preached. Ride this one out, and I believe your son will come back. If her church is the one, he may go there. That is a possibility.

I Was Embarrassed by My Daughter's Behavior . . .

Last night I went to a meeting without knowing that my daughter and her boy friend were going to be there. I sat a few rows behind them, and it was obvious they didn't know I was there. I was so embarrassed by their behavior. I thought I had raised my daughter to realize that displaying affection in public is in poor taste. Apparently I didn't. Obviously, she doesn't know how it looks to others. Do you have any suggestions as to how I could get this across to her?

Remember the little poem that went something like this: "Love is blind, but the neighbors ain't"? This is a common problem among young people. They become all wrapped up in themselves and forget others are around. They aren't doing anything evil intentionally, nor do they intend to embarrass anyone. Also, today's young people see sexuality more overtly expressed than we did at their age. I'm not condoning this—to me it is also a problem. I, too, am embarrassed by some of the things I see. Other young people are also embarrassed. They don't like to see this in other kids—they think it's "uncool."

Compare today's young people with kids of the '50s. I'd say kids are generally less affectionate in public today than they were then. The book of Ecclesiastes talks about a time and a place for everything, and that's fact. There is the matter of appropriateness involved here. You say your daughter was with her boy friend at a Christian meeting—that's good, but their behavior was not good.

I'm concerned that there was no feedback in your letter. If you had talked to her, perhaps your letter would have been different. You indicate you're wondering what to do. Perhaps you're afraid of your daughter—and you shouldn't be. Many parents are afraid of their children. Sit down with her and talk about this. Tell her how you feel and how you think it looks to others. She might reply, "Oh, mother, I didn't realize how it looked," or "It got out of hand." It often happens that the simplest answer is the best answer. I'm a great believer in face–

to–face confrontation, saying, "This is what I saw and this is how I felt. Perhaps you didn't mean it that way. Perhaps you were trying to do the right thing––or maybe you just didn't think. But you have to start thinking, you're a big girl now. . . ." This direct approach should help her to understand how you feel. Try the straight–on approach.

What Has Happened to Our Moral Standards?

Last Friday I went through a shattering experience. My daughter's school newspaper ran a factual first person article in which a student described her sexual misadventures and the frustrating time she had trying to obtain a morning–after pill. The paper ran an accompanying editorial condemning the school for not providing adequate sexual information. The editorial said it is just as important for students to be aware of their sexuality as it is to pass a test on the U.S. Constitution! When I was growing up, there was a right way to live and a wrong way––and every young person knew the difference. Now it seems there are no moral standards to go by.

I agree, it does seem that way. This is probably the result of one of the limitations of the democratic experiment: we've tried to build a secular cult in America. We want to be fair to all people of all views. Now you and I happen to be in the dominant (or what was the dominant) Christian segment of that culture. We feel that our school system is just that, a system, and should express this dominant opinion. However, our courts and those who have attempted to deal with this problem have decided that there ought to be a separation of church and state. Most of us, having thought about this a good deal, have decided that separation of church and state is one of our really prime heritages. We can see the problems when the dominant culture begins to exert itself; when we agree with it, it's good —when we disagree, it's bad. The concept that brought our country into existence is really based on this issue.

Specifically in your letter, we're talking about our kids in school and sex education. It's difficult for me to believe that any school superintendent, principal, or teacher desires to get into the kind of controversy that develops over sex education. This is a difficult matter for these people. They have to face differences of opinion and tremendous pressures as a result. Some parents feel their children ought to have sex education, and some feel it has no place in the school curriculum at all. I doubt that many principals and superintendents take this on willingly. The school has accepted this duty out of necessity.

Many students never go to our churches. The school officials see the tremendous spiritual and moral void in the lives of these young people. Mistakenly, in my opinion, they have thought you could fill the spiritual and moral void with more specific information about sex—more biological information. I don't think the problem can be solved with biology.

I do think that your question points out the urgent necessity of integrating all this biological information with spiritual and moral guidance from the home and from the church. I believe the home and church must step into this issue with both feet. To the degree that we shirk our responsibility in the home and church, the schools will be forced to fill the gap. The schools are handicapped because you cannot talk about sexuality separate from morals. It isn't a biological issue—it is a spiritual and moral issue. And the schools are supposed to stay clear of these areas.

My Daughter Isn't a Virgin . . .

You'll probably say I was wrong for looking in my daughter's diary, but it was lying there open, so I looked. I couldn't be-

lieve it—I still can't. I hope it was all her imagination, but if it isn't, then my daughter isn't living the pure life I thought she was. She isn't a virgin anymore, and I don't even know her boy friend's name. I'm sick about it. Do I confront her with it, or hint about it, or just believe what she tells me? She's just out of high school and I've even thought about asking her to leave the house.

I'm troubled that you even considered asking your daughter to leave the house. It's hard to conceive that any good could be accomplished going to that extreme. Think about it from a Christian point of view—aren't you happy that the Lord doesn't ask you to leave the house because of your sins? Rather, He says, "Come unto me."

What about looking into your daughter's diary? I imagine many mothers would have been tempted in the same way. I do wonder why your daughter left the diary open with that kind of information in it. It's very possible she subconsciously wanted you to read it. Perhaps she wanted you to know about her situation and is looking for help. Maybe she felt tremendous guilt. She may also be looking for some advice.

One of the most wonderful things about being a Christian is that when we confess our sins, our God is faithful and just to forgive us our sins, and to cleanse us from all unrighteousness. We humans tend to "grade" sins. Sexual sins such as adultery are at the serious end along with murder and robbery. Then gossip and lying fall somewhere at the other end as less serious. It is difficult for us to believe that God will forgive sexual sins as readily as He will the so-called lesser sins. If your daughter has indeed committed fornication, surely the love of Christ is not too limited to cover that sin. Don't sell God's forgiveness short. Your daughter can probably accept God's forgiveness, if she is forgiven by her mother.

I think you should confront your daughter regarding this matter. Tell her you were in her room and saw the diary open, and were tempted to read it. Tell her of your concern. She may be contrite and want to find forgiveness. In that case, point her to the Lord. Use the opportunity to talk to her as you should have talked before. Use this as a wonderful open door to communication. It is possible for God to take this "grain of sand" experience in your life and turn it into a pearl!

What's Sex for Anyway?

A few days ago my teen-age son and I were talking about dating. Happily, my son is both a committed Christian and an honest thinker. Recently he's been concerned about the physical relationship developing between his girl friend and him. They've been going together for two years now. He shared with me some of the questions on his mind. Frankly, I was impressed with the quality of my son's relationship with the girl. They love each other as friends as well as man and woman. I believe it is a healthy and beneficial thing for both of them. Anyway, we were discussing pretty openly the struggle all young couples go through. More or less jokingly he asked, "What's sex for anyway?" Well, it stuck with me. It seems to me that God could have avoided a lot of problems by coming up with another method of perpetuating the race. Sex seems to have become such a big deal lately. It makes one wonder—why did God make us male and female in the first place?

The complete and total answer to your question can be found only in the mind of God Himself. However, we do have a good number of hints in the Bible as to His purpose. There is in man an incompleteness when he is left alone—whether separate from God or from other people. In this incompleteness of man without woman, and woman without man, there is a hint as to man's nature. Man by himself is indeed incomplete. He can only know fullness and completeness in relationships with others. He is a social being—he must have relationships. God has built into man not only the need for relationships, but He has made him a sexual being. This sexual drive causes him to seek wholeness or completeness in a particular way.

Perhaps there are some single people reading these words. They're wondering, "Does that mean I'll never be complete without being married?" Is a single person destined to incompleteness? In a certain sense, this is true. A single person does

141

miss the blessing of "completeness" to be found in marriage. However, a perceptive unmarried person can often learn more about life and have a more rewarding life than an insensitive married person.

Keep in mind that God instituted home life in this way. God was a Father before we were fathers. Christ was a Son before we were sons. Life is built on relationships. In this sense I believe sexuality is a gift of God. It is given to show us that our search for wholeness and completeness takes place in relationship to Him and with one another. I think I understand your son's question in this respect. In our modern culture we have made the mistake of believing that the only way two people of the opposite sex can relate to each other is sexually. This is a myth that needs to be exploded. Be thankful for your son's perceptiveness and maturity.

How Do I Talk to My Sons about Sex?

I have two sons, fourteen and sixteen. I desperately want to talk to them about dating, marriage, and sex because I feel it is important for them to have a biblical perspective. We've never talked about this sort of thing before, since I'm from a rather conservative background. But I know it may be too late if I don't approach the subject soon. How do I go about it? Should I talk to them one at a time—or together? Should my wife be there, too? How do you get started? I certainly don't want to blow my opportunity to be a good Christian father.

You mention you want to get started before it is too late. In a sense you are already "too late," if too late is the right designation. By the time he is fourteen or sixteen, a boy has been introduced to most of the biological facts about sex. He's learned these things from his friends, picking up information here and there. He has had discussions in school and in Sunday school. So from a biological viewpoint, his sexuality has been pretty well established in his mind.

However, the most important aspect of sexual understanding is not biological. The biology comes about more or less naturally, as you're well aware. The whole area of social responsibilities in sexuality is something else. Apparently, from what you have said, an open confrontation on this subject would be difficult for you. I can hardly conceive of your doing that. However, there are some tremendous tools available to us today that would help you get into this matter. With the junior high children we have used a tape by Dr. James Dobson, author of *Dare to Discipline*. One side of the tape is designed for parents, the other for children. As the children listen by themselves, they may stop the tape and replay certain sections. Afterwards, you should give them an opportunity to ask questions about these matters.

Dr. Dobson deals pretty much with the biological aspects of sex. A tape or book conveying that aspect from a Christian point of view is excellent. However, in the area of social responsibility, there are two books which I recommend for young people of fourteen to eighteen. They are both written by a fine Presbyterian pastor named Charlie Shedd. One is *Letters to Karen*, and the other, *Letters to Philip*. He writes one to his daughter and one to his son. Your boys should read *Letters to Philip*. After they have read the book, discuss it with them, perhaps a chapter at a time. Ask them, "How do you feel about this chapter? Did you understand what the author was saying?" You might find Dr. Shedd's book a guide to conversation to get you through the material you want to cover. It will give you a chance for some honest and open communication with your sons. This is how I would answer your question.

Sex Is Running Rampant in Our World . . .

There is so much permissiveness in the world in the area of sex. Yet nothing is being said regarding will power and discipline in everyday life. If only young people would practice self–discipline and self–control, if only they would have themselves for marriage! What heartaches they would avoid, not to mention spiritual and financial unhappiness, and guilt. What with the lenient abortion laws and increasing pressure on girls to wear revealing clothes, there is no wonder this problem of sex is running rampant. It is demoralizing America. What can we do about our teen–agers' preoccupation with sex?

You are saying some things with which all of us agree. There is an undue preoccupation with sex, and young people do need self–discipline. Chastity is vital to the fabric of our society. Saving oneself for marriage *would* avoid a lot of heartaches. What you have said is true. One of the things I am trying to do in this book is to bridge the gap between what we wish were true and what is true. Rather than simply stating what ought to happen, I am trying to show people how to make it happen.

The truth is our young people are caught up in a sex–saturated society. They are being manipulated by tremendously powerful forces in the media world. In every area of the advertising and entertainment industries there is a certain permissive spirit. It is more than permissiveness. It is a concerted, well-planned attack on the moral standards of the past. We are faced with a new morality, a "situation ethics" approach to crucial issues. This relativism raises havoc in our families, our lives, and our culture.

On the other hand, I must admit that our overreacting is also a problem. Some of the new morality is the result of people overreacting against people. For example, the Puritan attitude toward sex was an overreaction against certain practices of that period of history. We must find a balanced position in which we acknowledge that sex is God's idea, a gift from God.

Sex is sanctified! It becomes bad only when it is taken out of the context of marriage, when it is out of control. Be very careful not to give Satan credit for something God engineered! Satan is completely sterile—he has no creative powers. He simply couldn't create anything as beautiful as sex. God created sex. Satan can only pervert it, bend it, twist it, and make it evil. We want our young people to have a positive attitude toward sex. They need to understand that their bodies are a gift from God. These bodies must be used with restraint and responsibility within our society.

Our Teen–age Daughter Wants to Have a Premarital Sexual Experience . . .

I hope you can help us with our teen–age daughter. She wants to have a sexual experience outside of marriage. She has been brought up on solid Bible teachings and is supposed to be a Christian. Yet she insists on sowing her wild oats. All our warnings go unheeded. Any suggestions?

You are facing a tough situation. I wonder how many parents know what is really going on in the lives of their teen-agers. Your relationship with your daughter must be unusual. Not many teen–age daughters would be this open with parents. Before getting to your main question, I'd like to comment on the phrase, "supposed to be a Christian." I am amazed at how many parents seem to feel that they can "regiment" a child into some sort of childhood conversion experience. They hope this will give their children "blanket coverage" for the rest of their lives. A child may have attended a certain class, or said some words to a Sunday school teacher, or gone forward at a revival meeting. This is supposed to place some sort of a protective wall around him, to insulate him. His conduct from that point on is supposed to be perfect.

I don't know whether your daughter is really a Christian or not. But I do know that there are a great many "church members" who have never been internally converted—who have never really given their hearts to Jesus. They have, rather, gone through some sort of well–meaning regimentation. All of us parents do this with our children. A wise person once said, "A man's mind changed by force was never changed at all." And a "childhood conversion" which has taken place within the strictures and coercions of parental pressure probably doesn't mean much to the child involved.

The work of conversion is the work of the Holy Spirit. Conversion takes place inside people—in the intimate inner areas of their lives. And so, your daughter may or may not be a Christian. This is the work of the Holy Spirit, and it can't necessarily be tied to some emotional experience you remember early in her life.

Now let's look at this matter of having a sexual experience outside of marriage. Any kind of sexual experience involves the whole person. What your daughter is really saying here is that she wants a partial sexual experience—a physical experience of some kind outside the marriage bond. The problem is there is no way to have a fragmented or partial experience. Whenever you have a sexual experience, it involves your whole life . . . your body, mind, spirit, and emotions. It affects every area of your life. Try to show her that this experience will affect her more profoundly than she thinks. Let me suggest two books that would greatly help a girl facing this temptation: *I Loved a Girl* by Walter Trobisch and *Letters to Karen* by Charles Shedd. Your daughter needs to face up to the implications of her decision, rethink her priorities.

I'm Really Getting Tired of All This Nonsense about Sex . . .

I'm really getting tired of hearing all this nonsense about sex from supposedly Christian leaders. Don't they read God's

*Word any more? I'm speaking particularly about the attitude
that says sex is a beautiful thing. First John 2:16 says, "For
all these worldly things, these evil desires—the craze for sex
. . . are not from God. They are from this evil world itself"
(Living Bible). Please, can you help me give my kids a proper
perspective on what the Bible really says about sex?*

Let me point out first of all that I probably fall into the
category of "supposedly Christian leaders." In general I agree
with the statement that "sex is a beautiful thing." It is a true
statement. Before you throw down this book in disgust, let me
immediately add that I also appreciate the sentiment behind
your letter. You are saying that you feel that the whole area
of sex has been perverted. Sexual sin is forbidden in the Bible.
In the writings of Paul especially we are urged to "flee" certain things: "fornication . . . youthful lusts . . ." (1 Cor.
6:18; 2 Tim. 2:22). These are biblical phrases.

Despite that you must also conclude that God is the One
who thought up sex in the first place! Genesis 1 tells us God
created man and woman—male and female. Paul also says
the marriage bed is undefiled. And the Song of Solomon is a
beautiful ode to marital love. Sex was God's idea! However,
the perversion of sex, the twisting of this good thing to make
it bad, was Satan's idea.

Our society has used God's great gift to sell things: a can
of motor oil being held up by a bikini-clad girl on a billboard.
What's the connection between a can of motor oil and a bikini? The obvious connection is you, the man, the viewer. You
probably don't even look at the can of oil! You'd rather look
at the bikini. That's because the sex drive is basic to man.

The attitude we are really considering and condemning is
the *world's* worship of sex as a beautiful thing. The world has
it out of context, outside marriage. What they are *saying* is
untrue. Within the marriage relationship, where God is the
Ordainer of the family and home, sex is a beautiful gift from
God. I do believe we need to protect our children from the
perversion of sex. But we also need to give them a positive
and open attitude about the body. It was created by God and
there's nothing wicked or dirty about it. In Colossians 3:17

Paul says, "And whatsoever ye do in word or deed, do all in the name of the Lord Jesus, giving thanks to God and the father by him." This applies to sex as well as to the other areas of life.

Our Daughter Is Engaged to a Non-Christian . . .

We have a problem that people just don't seem to understand. I'm hoping you will. Last month our daughter became engaged to a fellow she'd been dating for some time. They just came home one night and announced it. He's really a nice person —courteous, pleasant, intelligent. That's the problem—he's too nice. That's why no one, not even the people at church, understand why we're concerned. He's not a Christian—not as far as we can tell. Maybe we're old–fashioned, but doesn't the Bible say something about a Christian being not unequally yoked to an unbeliever? Whenever we mention this to our friends, they give us a strange look that seems to ask, "Don't you know a good deal when you see one?" We try to explain that no matter how nice a fellow is, if he isn't a born-again believer, he just can't be the spiritual leader in a home as he should be. The last time we mentioned this to our daughter, she became very upset and said something like "Frank may not be a spiritual leader, but when we're alone I can trust him, which is more than I can say for most of the guys at church." She's right, so what can we say?

I'm going to assume that what you have said in this letter is factual. I'm also accepting the inference behind what you have said: he is a nice young man; he does behave better than some of the boys at the church. That is a sad commentary on today's so–called "Christian" ethic—that a boy (even a Christian) may go as far as a girl will let him, that somehow or other it is the girl who has to draw the line.

So let's assume Frank is not a Christian. Then the practical problem is that your daughter does love him. They *are* engaged and they have decided to get married. In casting a question on your daughter's potential husband, you are beginning to drive a wedge between yourselves and your daughter. She will side with him because she feels your accusations are a reflection on her choice. The more you dwell on this, the deeper the chasm between you will grow.

May I suggest that you and your husband resist trying to do the work of the Holy Spirit! Begin to pray for this young man. Be the kind of loving, accepting Christian parents all of us want to be. Welcome the young man into your family. Show Christian grace toward him. As he goes in and out of your home, he will begin to experience Christ in your love for him. Pray that he will see that beyond all his fine behavior, he needs the Savior.

No matter how good he seems on the surface, deep down in his heart any man knows he has a personal need. Comparing himself to the other fellows at church isn't much of a challenge. But looking at Jesus revealed in you *will* be a challenge! Rather than drive a wedge between you and your daughter by being judgmental, let me encourage you to throw arms of love around your prospective son-in-law. Begin to see him as one for whom Christ died, rather than one who is taking your daughter away from you.

Our Son Wants to Move In with His Girl Friend . .

Our son thinks it is all right to move in with his girl friend before they marry. He says they won't do anything wrong—he promised! Both John and his fiancée profess to be Christians, but they seldom go to church. Please pray for them and tell me how to handle this situation.

We surely do need to pray for your son and his fiancée. Many other young people today are in this same situation.

Over the past few years there has been a startling erosion in the attitudes of young people toward this issue. For generations society has held that people should wait until after marriage to live together. Now the idea seems to be that you ought to try all these experiences before you marry, to see if it will work. Those who advocated pre-marital sex and trial marriage promised us better marital adjustment and stability in the home. Instead, the divorce rate is rising higher and higher. The whole institution of marriage is in jeopardy. This would lead me to think that our permissive attitude is heading us in the wrong direction.

Now about your son's promise not to do anything wrong. It is possible, of course, but highly improbable. You know that—and I suspect he and his girl friend do as well. Perhaps his suggestion is indicative of the relationship they are having already.

Unfortunately, many young people today tend to see marriage and the whole business of sex as simply a physical experience. They reduce it to that kind of an association—two bodies living in the same home, the sexual relationship merely physical. Their attitude is—what does it matter? According to the Bible and our experience, however, these relationships are not simply physical—they are emotional and spiritual as well. They affect us in deep and long-lasting ways. Using this kind of "logic," your son and his fiancée may be thinking they will just try it. If it doesn't work, then they'll forget it and try again with someone else.

The Word of God tells us there is more to this intimate relationship than that. We don't just walk away from it. Deep scars will remain. You know this already. That is why you wrote the letter. But your young people don't know it. There are books on the subject that may help them. Try to get them to read *Why Wait Until Marriage?* by Evelyn DuVal. They might also read Walter Trobisch's *I Loved a Girl*.

College:
Part Seven.
To Go or Not to Go?

Should a Parent Influence His Son's Choice of Occupation?

How much should a parent try to influence his son's choice of a career? My son would make a wonderful minister, and I'm tempted to launch a campaign to push him in that direction. I've considered introducing him to especially sharp ministers. I've also thought about inviting seminary students over to our house so he can see how interesting they are. He really doesn't know what he wants to do with his life, but he says right now he'd like to be a drama teacher. I just think such a career would be a waste of the talents God has given him. What do you think?

I'm glad you are ready to push but haven't started pushing! Don't start. You could do some irreparable damage. For one thing, the idea that ministers should be recruited or pushed into the ministry frightens me. People should not be "pushed" into any occupation, particularly this one. A Christian minister is "called." God must speak by His Holy Spirit to that person. If a person can do anything else with his life, and be happy doing it, he should do that. One should be a minister only if this is the only thing he can do! A minister must be called of God. He cannot *become* a minister because of some whim. It's not a matter of being recruited—Uncle Sam pointing with his finger says, "I want you." And young men join the army during a momentary spurt of patriotism. The ministry isn't like that.

Most people enter certain occupations because they are familiar with them. Perhaps they've had a pleasant experience or have met an unusual person in a certain occupation. Many a young man has gone into the ministry after reading the life of D. L. Moody or Charles H. Spurgeon—or Billy Graham. The story of John and Betty Stam, or the five martyred missionaries to Ecuador, has inspired others to go to the mission field. All this is good.

But parents shouldn't push! First of all, it would be too obvious to your son. It would probably become counter–productive and might even boomerang on you. Second, it might bring about something outside the will of God. You mention drama. I don't agree that this would be a waste. Several of my friends are in the business of producing plays or Christian films. As I have looked at the life and ministry of one of these men, I would guess that more people have come to Christ as a result of his films than through the efforts of many evangelists combined. While this is hard to believe, perhaps, the effectiveness of good drama should not be minimized. Christian films, in particular, have been greatly used of God.

Why Do We View Drinking As Wrong?

Our oldest son has just turned eighteen. He is about to leave for college in another city. Yesterday he asked me a question that really floored me. Now I feel I must give him some sort of answer before he leaves home. Here is his question: Why do churches view drinking as wrong? He says he can see how excessive drinking relates to the stewardship of our bodies. He recognizes that drunkenness could cost him the respect of those around him and endanger their lives. But he wants to know what is wrong with social drinking if you keep control of yourself. To tell the truth, I couldn't think of a single biblical reason why he shouldn't drink. Would you help me out?

Let's start with your first question—why do churches view drinking as wrong? Most churches and clergymen do view drinking as wrong simply because the church has to deal with the results of drinking. Churches see people whose lives are out of control financially, or whose marriages and other family relationships are ruined because of drink. Many churches and Christians in social work have concluded that alcohol is too great a problem to ignore. Alcoholism is one of the greatest problems confronting our world today. It is the leading so-called drug problem, and it is moving down into the high school and junior high levels at an alarming rate.

I could, of course, skirt one of the aspects of your question. Do I have biblical reasons for my convictions? It reminds me of the question the Pharisees asked Jesus: "Is it lawful to give tribute to Caesar, or not?" (Matt. 22:17). Jesus replied "Show me the tribute money. . . . Whose is this image?" (vv. 19,20). He then added, "Render therefore unto Caesar the things which are Caesar's; and unto God the things that are God's" (v. 21).

I would prefer not to be forced into a position between being a Christian and advocating social drinking. Can you build a biblical argument for total abstinence? Many Christians are tee-totalers. I happen to be one, and I plan to stay that way. I do not see the value of drinking. In fact, I would come at the matter from the opposite direction—why drink? What's the value? I can't find a compelling logic for it. I look at society and can't see one redeeming value for social drinking. You hear about the tax revenue that comes from the drinking public. Compare the revenue with the cost of drunkenness and alcoholism to society, and you will find it to be a losing proposition.

Many people feel a social drink makes them less inhibited, more lucid and interesting. Listen to a tape of the dialogue at a cocktail party. It would reveal that the conversation becomes increasingly more boring; the volume rises but the logic goes down. Such a study reveals anything but a pretty picture.

I'm opposed to alcohol because of what it does to people and to our society. But I agree, your son would have a hard time building an argument for total abstinence on the basis of a specific verse in the Bible. Emphasize the value and the importance of one's fellow man and society. That teaching you *can* find in the Bible, and that is my basis for opposing the drinking of alcoholic beverages.

Our Daughter Wants to Go Away to College . . .

Our daughter will be graduating from high school in June and will be going to college in the fall. She wants to go to a college in another town so she can get away from home. My wife and I want her to attend a private college in our town and live at home for at least a couple of years. This will save us money and give her a chance to mature. She wants to go to one of our state universities, but we've heard a lot of stories about the students there. Are we wrong in wanting her to stay at home?

No, I don't think you're wrong for wanting your daughter to stay at home. This is a normal desire for any parent. We want to hang on to our children just a little longer, to enjoy them just a few more years. To protect and prepare them just a little longer. However, I do think you would be wrong to *insist* that she stay at home. You could be robbing her of an important experience. She needs a chance to grow up.

There is a time when every person must "leave the nest." Every child must try his own wings. Your daughter is not saying you have a bad home, or that she dislikes you. She is saying that she is normal. Should you insist that she be tied to your "apron strings"? All normal children need the opportunity to go out and gain experience on their own. Isn't it amazing how well most of them do?

Your daughter wants to go to college in another town. You want her to stay home. Let us look at the dangers in staying home. Over the past ten years many questions have come to me from parents who are frustrated by their children from seventeen to twenty-one. These young people are living at home and going to community colleges. What happens? The young person lives at home and goes to school during the day. He or she has a car. There are activities at school in the evening, and the young person comes in at odd hours. This causes strain at home.

What about the young person who goes away to college? You might ask that same frustrated parent, "What's your son doing?" The answer would be: "Oh, he's studying, cramming. . . ." Actually, that son may be out until five in the morning. He might be doing all sorts of things outside your knowledge. And that's the point I'm making. If he's home and going to school, then you see and become a part of his problems. That causes unnecessary anxiety on your part.

In your case, I'd suggest a compromise. Consider allowing your daughter to live in the dormitory of the private college in your home town. This would give her a certain amount of freedom, but it would allow you to exercise a certain amount of control. Thus she could spend time with her friends outside the home, but she would be close at hand. This might be your answer.

Remember this. Just because she stays at home where you can observe her problems doesn't mean that her problems will be any less or any different than those of other young people. Thousands have these same problems and survive them beautifully, even though their parents aren't there to observe it all!

We're Worried about Our Daughter and Her Boy Friend Together at College . . .

My wife and I have four children. All four have gone through a time of rebellion against me, my values, and my religious training. The three older ones have grown beyond this and are living clean, wholesome lives. Our youngest will be going to college this fall and she insists on going to the school her boy friend attends. We're afraid that when they are together away from family influence and on a secular campus, they might become too heavily involved with each other. They might do something they'd regret later. Our dilemma? Should we let her go to this school or should we insist that she go to another school, perhaps the junior college in our town?

You should have a pretty high level of confidence at this point. You're showing a 75 percent success factor! What you're teaching your children must be pretty sound, because they seem to return to it. However, the way you are applying these truths must be faulty in some way. I wonder why all four became rebellious. It's possible your children are just this way, but I wonder if you are perhaps too rigid. Though they respect your teachings, they rebel against your methods. Maybe you've been too authoritarian. I believe in *authority,* but *authoritarianism* is something else.

By this time your daughter has already established her own value system. Going away to college probably isn't going to change anything a great deal. Your fears are the fears of every parent who ever had a daughter . . . that your child will ignore your teaching and the solid foundation you've laid. Will she reject the Word of God she has learned at home, in Sunday school, and church? In spite of your prayers and concern, will she, in an unguarded instant, go off and do something irresponsible? Unfortunately, that's one of the risks you take—along with the rest of us parents! It is well worth taking because of the rewards, however.

Think of the blessing of having a child who lives out your trust—who becomes the kind of person you want him or her to be. Three of your four children are living clean, wholesome lives. That must be a great reward. I'd advise you to trust God for the 100 percent in this case.

I would suggest some give and take, some open discussion. Whatever decision is made, you and your daughter must come together on it. Share your opinions with her, but listen to her side of it. Then arrive at a decision that takes into consideration the best of both sides.

Bibliography

Caring Enough to Confront, David Augsburger; Glendale: Regal Books, 1973.

Dare to Discipline, James Dobson; Wheaton: Tyndale, 1972.

Hide and Seek, James Dobson; Old Tappan, N.J., 1974.

Why Wait Until Marriage?, Evelyn Duvall; New York: Association Press, 1965.

I Never Promised You a Disneyland, Jay Kesler with Tim Stafford; Waco: Word, 1975.

Outside Disneyland, Jay Kesler with Tim Stafford; Waco: Word, 1977.

An Ounce of Prevention, Bruce Narramore; Grand Rapids: Zondervan, 1973.

Help! I'm a Parent, Bruce Narramore; Grand Rapids: Zondervan, 1975.

Letters to Karen, Charlie Shedd; Nashville: Abingdon, 1965.

Letters to Philip, Charlie Shedd; Old Tappan, N.J.: Revell, 1969.

I Loved a Girl, Walter Trobisch; New York: Harper and Row Jubilee, 1975.

I Married You, Walter Trobisch; New York: Harper and Row, 1971.

Love Is a Feeling to Be Learned, Walter Trobisch; Downer's Grove: Inter-Varsity Press, 1968.

Jay Kesler is president of Youth for Christ International. He has been associated with YFC for more than two decades, and was elected president in 1973. Jay and his wife have three children: Laura, Bruce, and Terri. They make their home in West Chicago, Illinois.

Other Books by Jay Kesler:
  Let's Succeed with Our Teenagers
  I Never Promised You a Disneyland (with
    Tim Stafford)
  Outside Disneyland (with Tim Stafford)